The Gentle Touch

Ardeth Greene Kapp

Deseret Book Company   Salt Lake City, Utah   1978

Library of Congress Cataloging in Publication Data

Kapp, Ardeth Greene, 1931-
   The gentle touch.

   1. Teaching.   2. Slow learning children.   I. Title.
LB1025.2.K347   371.1'02   78-12747
ISBN 0-87747-724-8

To my parents,
Edwin Kent Greene and June Leavitt Greene

With deep appreciation for their teaching their children "to understand the doctrine of repentance, faith in Christ the Son of the living God, and of baptism and the gift of the Holy Ghost." (D&C 68:25.) And particularly for their patience, love, and discipline as they have shown me the way in my "second estate," so that we might anticipate a continuation of our precious relationship for ever and ever.

Acknowledgments

Grateful appreciation is expressed to many friends, including Wm. James Mortimer, Lowell M. Durham, Jr., and Eleanor Knowles for their words of encouragement in my writing efforts; to my husband, Heber, who listens carefully and improves my endeavors with his perceptive suggestions; to my sister, Sharon Larsen, and her daughter Shelly, who are the source of inspiration for several of the stories and much more; to Judy Smith, my dear friend who reviewed the manuscript and refined it considerably; to Emily Watts, who assisted with the proofreading and editing; and to Michael Clane Graves for his thoughtful attention to the graphic design of *The Gentle Touch*.

And finally, I am especially grateful to my many students, whose names in the stories in some cases have been changed out of respect for their privacy, but who taught me much as I endeavored to teach them using a gentle touch.

Contents

Preface

A good tool misused or applied out of time can be a destructive force. I believe that it is through the teacher's sensitivity that each child is guarded and protected against the misuse of even good teaching methods and techniques.

I believe that only as there is unity in the mind and in the heart of the teacher can the teaching methods be safely used. While working with student teachers, I discovered the ease with which skills and concepts can be taught and learned and even recited back in the words of the experts; but this response usually comes as a result of the student teachers working with their minds, not their hearts.

I believe that if a teacher is ever to be allowed into the private, sacred realm of a child's heart, where lasting changes take place and lasting imprints are made, a sensitivity to the inner spirit of each child and a reverence for teaching moments is required. This sensitivity is difficult to teach, but is unquestionably the most important quality to be learned.

After many approaches, I finally realized that if I could just take these student teachers with me, so to speak, by recreating actual moments of learning with the accuracy that would allow them to feel for themselves not necessarily what I felt, but what they felt within their own hearts, minds, and souls, then they could safely use their own gifts and be trusted to touch and mold a child's character.

I wonder why it is that the sense of smell can return a total experience to the consciousness even better, I think, than sight or sound. It is in the recollection of that smell of chalk dust; warm, sweaty bodies after recess; school lunch; and poster paint that even the emotion of a teaching experience not recalled for years is relived with such clarity as though it were occurring for the first time.

Having experienced the feeling of these teaching moments, dedicated student teachers can begin to let go, to open up, to experience the miracle of teaching with their entire beings. Then, as if by magic, in their own classrooms they are able to lay their teaching tools close by for ready access and, with their eyes and hearts wide open, begin to feel their way carefully along the path. With this feeling, they begin to accept and care for each child according to his particular need, and then pause just long enough to humbly rejoice in the result.

Having realized some benefit from sharing with others what have become valuable teaching moments, I wish now to share them with you—with parents, with teachers, and with all who may desire increased awareness as they approach with reverence each teaching moment.

A Little Visit

It was the beginning of another school year, and I had just received the roll card for my class. I quickly scanned the list of names, hoping to make some association with as many as possible, thus trying to avoid having anyone be just a name on a page, even for the first day. As I reviewed the permanent record of each child, refusing to be concerned about any negative comments at this point, my anticipation and excitement grew. I knew what could be accomplished in the life of each student during the coming year. I had already sequenced the lesson manuals and determined the rate of progress required to reach the goals I had set. I then marked the calendar accordingly in carefully measured portions.

Thus prepared, I stood at the door to Room 16 at 8:30 the morning of the first day of school and anxiously awaited the arrival of those who would bring with them varied interests, needs, abilities, and personalities that would combine together in a magnificent human kaleidoscope, if handled with a gentle touch.

As I watched at the door, they entered one by one, each adding to the group, which would spend the major portion of the day together during the next nine months. The girls were in the colorful print dresses, many of them accented with crisp white collars. The boys had their plaid shirts tucked into their bluejeans, which bunched together at the waist. The jeans were often held in place by too-long belts adjusted with homemade holes in an attempt to accommodate the discrepancy between the waist of the boy and the size of the pants. Of course, there were some exceptions, but in outward appearance there was much conformity.

I don't know if a teacher ever gets over the mixed emotions, anticipation, burden of responsibility, self-evaluation, and expectation that all flood together during the few seconds it takes to walk to the front of the room and begin to establish that relationship between teacher and student with a new class for the first time. I could hear my heart pounding as I walked up the aisle. My goals for the year were clearly in mind: to see that every child felt good about himself, and, with increased confidence, had opportunities for reaching his potential. I had the material, the lesson plans, and the preparation. Now I had the students to make up the class. As I reached the front of the room I folded my arms, dropped them, clasped my hands, and finally reached for the security of a book, which I held in front of me.

As I looked into the eager faces of the children, all eyes were on me, and I felt as though they were watching a bird ready to spread its wings for its first solo flight. To avoid interrupting this moment of anticipation, I resisted my plan for an enthusiastic welcome and remained silent, responding only with a sincere smile as I took time to make eye contact with each child.

Something in that incident caused me to feel ill-at-ease with the introduction I had planned. Questions in the form of challenges came flooding into my mind. Was it my goals, my plans, my desires, my needs that these sensitive, trusting children were to bring to pass?

I looked into each face, beyond the external physical features, for that insight so often revealed through the eyes (if one looks carefully with enough empathy) to establish a trust and then receive in return a steady gaze. In that moment I felt the necessity to know and understand these children better, not so much as a class but rather as individuals, and ever so quickly my goals for the year seemed wanting, in need of reevaluation. It was not my place to mold clay to conform to a design of my making. I must first know something of the material with which I might work.

I looked at one little girl whose name was printed neatly on a card in front of her desk. Kathy, I thought, how do you feel? What are you wanting to accomplish? What are your dreams, your goals, your fears, and your concerns? Kathy, I said to myself, if I take time to listen, will you trust me, and tell me, and then allow me to help you to get a vision of your possibilities so that together we can work for your success? Will you, Kathy? Will you tell me what you are thinking?

While waiting for an answer to the question that was never spoken, I remembered a friend of mine who told me about how the forces of her entire neighborhood were marshaled in search of her missing four-year-old. All of the nearby places had been searched and now, with increased concern and anxiety, a wider radius for investigation had been determined. It was the little boy's mother who, in desperation, walked many blocks from home, across the freeway, through an open field, and finally caught sight of her little son standing by a fence. With his arm stretched to its full length through the fence, he was enraptured by the feel of a horse on the other side, licking his hand. The mother, caught between her relief and her pent-up emotions, grabbed the child by one arm and anxiously inquired, "Bradley, what's wrong with you?" The full explanation for his conduct was given in his simple response. "Mom," he said in a pleading voice, "all the time I need a pony and I don't have one."

I thought again of my class. Maybe if I could learn the needs of Kathy, and of Jim and Bradley and Susan, if I could find them and discover their needs, then their sometimes questionable behavior might seem much more understandable. As teachers we may not always be able to provide the ponies, but if we try, we can better understand the needs of a child.

And so that year began with a different approach than was planned—it began with a visiting schedule. It might have been called an interview, a conference, or a report session, but the word *visit* seemed to best describe our purpose. It was during these little visits that I began to discover the quality, the tenderness, the limitation, and above all the sacredness of the material that was entrusted in part to my keeping during that school year.

The first visit with a child usually began with the simple question, "How do you enjoy school?" Although the response was usually very brief, the shrug of the shoulders, the smile on the face, or the fidgeting of the fingers revealed much. One child in response to the question might take a deep breath and never stop talking, as if he would have exploded had the teacher not asked the question. Another child might fidget in his seat and duck his head, hoping you would go on and not wait for an answer. And so for that child, the first question, unanswered, was followed quickly by the next, "How can I help you?" Often the response to such an inquiry would suggest that the child had never considered the possibility of a teacher actually being a help, and judging from the reaction of some of the students, that possibility seemed quite unlikely.

After a level of trust had been established, through careful listening and genuine concern, it was possible to be privileged on occasion to have entrance into the very hearts of those I hoped to teach. It was in these moments that the sacredness of teaching became evident as I was admitted into places of reverence.

During these little visits, the students would often tell me things they might otherwise hope to keep from a teacher. "Mrs. Kapp, I'm dumb in

math," Julie confessed, and after such a declaration
it seemed that she was laying down a burden much
too heavy for the size of the problem. "Julie," I
asked, "is that something you would like me to help
you with?" Her response seemed almost one of surprise, as though being "dumb in math" was like being doomed from birth. She nodded, so I wrote by
her name in my book the date and a comment that
became a commitment for me to help Julie with
math. After that agreement, my efforts to assist her
seemed not to be that of a teacher prodding, but
hopefully of a friend following through on a promise
made.

Finally one day, as I once again worked a problem through on the board, trying hard to communi-
cate, Julie's countenance changed. The strain on her
face was gone, replaced by an expression of joy mingled with surprise. "What happened, Julie?" I asked,
to which she excitedly replied, "Finally you said it
right!" I felt my burden lightened and then
wondered how it might have been without the insight from our visit.

Another day, Billy was asked to remain after
school. At the first opportunity I reminded him that
he'd been daydreaming the entire day and that his
lessons were not completed, and I continued, "If you
don't accept some responsibility . . ." It was immediately apparent that he was still far removed
from the matter of my concern, so before I could unload my anxiety for his total lack of cooperation during the day, I thought it best to have a little visit.

"Billy," I said, in a quieter tone, since the louder

approach did not penetrate his contemplation, "what do you think about as you sit there all day in a world of your own?"

As though I had spoken to him for the first time that day, his eyes met mine and he opened his heart: "Well, you see, Mrs. Kapp, I'm the pitch on our Little League team, and last week we lost our game. On Saturday we play again, and I just kept thinking and thinking about what I can do. We just gotta win."

Being allowed access to his inner thoughts, I found my own priorities wavering and interest changing as I asked with genuine concern, "Billy, can I help in any way?" After some time I learned of his obsession to be a professional ball player. We talked about the long road ahead, the discipline, the determination, and the preparation. We talked about playing ball in high school and college, and being at the top. I remained silent while allowing him to dream, until the time seemed right to bring him back to reality. "Billy," I asked, with a bit of a smile, "how will you make it to college?" He responded with a smile. "Doing that stuff," he said, lowering his hand with dirty knuckles on top of his books. Together we made an agreement that he would take his lessons home and do them that night.

As he left, I felt some satisfaction in having won that inning. My thoughts were interrupted a moment later when he popped his head through the door again and exclaimed, "Mrs. Kapp, if you could come to our game tomorrow and watch me play, I think that would help!" I agreed to be there.

It was during another visit that I discovered my

assumptions could have completely misled me. Becky enjoyed school, did well, and had many friends. She was consistently well-prepared and always looked neat and tidy. Even at the end of the school day, her dress was spotless and her hair in place. As we visited, I admired her meticulous appearance. "Becky," I finally said, "is there anything you would like to do to make school even more enjoyable?" Immediately she responded, "I keep hoping and hoping you'll choose me to take the chalk brushes outside and clean them, but you just always choose the boys." And then, in a pleading tone, she added, "Won't it ever be my turn?" Immediately I pictured this immaculate little girl in a cloud of chalk dust and thought, No, Becky, without this little visit it would never have been your turn. How could I have possibly imagined that cleaning those dirty brushes could be an enviable task to someone like you? Looking into her bright eyes, I responded, "Yes, Becky, it will be your turn all next week starting on Monday." Then I wrote a note by her name in my book. The expression on her face gave me the impression that she was finally being rewarded for all her past efforts to please the teacher. As she left my desk, I thought of the likelihood of this child never having had that special privilege (according to her) of cleaning the brushes, just because the teacher assumed it was a boy's job.

I discovered, after about the first month, that it was the students who kept track of the schedule for their little visits, and it was from these visits that the goals for the class were set: their goals, their needs, their special interests, and their accomplishments. Fall slipped away, and winter, and then spring. The days on the new calendar prepared each month by the students were regularly marked off. Somehow, almost miraculously, as I reflected again on my goals for the year, they were not only accomplished, but surpassed.

A Safe Place

An old water-soaked raft was anchored securely a short distance from the shore at the Okinagan Lake. When a storm blew in, as one occasionally did, the raft remained in place, held by the cables that secured its position. We had come to the lake early that day, but gradually the sun had inched its way across the cloudless sky, until now the gentle, cool evening breeze brought ripples on the water's surface.

Since early morning, I had watched off and on the activities surrounding the raft. It seemed to be the center of attention for all those at play, as well as those who observed. The younger children swarmed all over the raft—standing, sitting with legs hanging over the edge dangling in the water, kneeling, shoving, pushing and yelling, into the water and out, again and again, seeming never to tire until all possibilities of the raft had been explored and discovered. Only then did they begin looking for new challenges to hold their attention and invite their interests. The older children had long since left the raft to find adventure some distance away; first to the rugged rocky cliffs, with several huge boulders jutting out of the water; then beyond the pier, around the point, and finally almost out of sight.

Now I watched the younger children with particular interest. Once the challenge of the raft had been conquered and they seemed to feel secure and confident, the raft served another purpose: not so much something to play on, or even near, but rather a safe place to return to. With the binoculars, I had enjoyed an occasional close-up of the expressions on the faces of these little sun-browned children who were turning even browner in the hot summer sun, assisted by its reflection on the water.

Jenny seemed to be one of the more adventuresome members of the group, but she was also that way in other situations. The challenge of the water was no different. I watched her hanging on the edge of the raft with one hand as she looked toward a boulder some distance away. As she let go and began to swim, I calculated the distance to the boulder and wondered about her intent. She took only a few strokes, then turned to quickly locate the raft and return to safety. This process continued as she inched out a little further each time, turning frequently to verify the location of her safety before venturing ahead. It became evident that knowing unquestionably the location of the raft provided the security and confidence that allowed her to venture further and further away. I watched her confidence grow each time she would master the extended distance and then return to safety.

Finally, having tried and tested her ability and confidence in measured amounts, Jenny returned once more to the raft, and climbed upon it to rest awhile, still looking toward the huge boulder some distance away. At times she seemed distracted briefly by the activities of the others as they enjoyed the security and safety of the raft, but then she would appear to measure again the distance from where she was to where she obviously intended to go. But now I, too, was measuring the distance, calculating her courage and anticipating the outcome. Finally she jumped off the raft, making a big splash and attracting everyone's attention. This time it was hand over hand in steady rhythm, never hesitating once to look back until she climbed up on the big boulder near the rock cliffs that marked her goal. Immediately she displayed her sense of victory as she waved to her friends on the raft, and they waved in return.

I thought about the importance of the raft in Jenny's accomplishment. Suppose it had not been anchored well. Suppose its location had changed according to every wind that blew. Suppose it was floating beneath the water's surface just out of sight at a time when she was checking back to secure her location. What then might have been the outcome? Pondered only briefly, the thought slipped away unanswered.

It was months later during a parent-teacher conference that the day at the lake returned to my mind with greater meaning. I had learned as a teacher to begin the conference by asking each parent how I might be of help, since my role was to assist the parent in his responsibility, rather than the parent accounting to me, the teacher.

One particular parent, Mrs. Olsen, didn't hesitate. As if she had rehearsed what she had in mind to say, she began, "You've probably noticed Linda is a little clinging vine, and you probably think we baby her at home, but honestly we don't." Without waiting for my response she continued. "Her brother and sisters are much older, and since she's the only one left at home, it's almost as if she were an only child. So you can understand how anxious we are that we help her to be independent and confident, but our efforts seem to be in vain." Almost as if to justify herself she added, "I'm always encouraging Linda by telling her she can do it, that she can work it out, that she can make decisions; and then her father and I move out and let her do it so she'll know we have confidence in her. We hope that she'll learn not to rely on us for every decision or expect us to do things for her that she can do for herself." Mrs. Olsen hesitated briefly, then continued, "We've really tried to not stand too close and smother her by being overprotective. We keep trying to move away to allow her to develop a little self-confidence, but as you can see, the harder we try, the more insecure she seems to be."

With a tone of anxiousness, Mrs. Olsen shifted the conversation and asked, "How does she get along at school?"

That very day while I was on playground duty, Linda had clung to my arm when I had let go of her hand and had put my hand in my pocket, hoping to encourage her to leave my side and join the others at four-square or tetherball.

To acknowledge the problem and share the concern of Mrs. Olsen was of little value unless I could suggest some possible solution, or at least some insight that might help the situation and encourage the mother. While searching for an answer, I heard Mrs. Olsen's words again in my mind, "We keep trying to move away to allow her to develop a little self-confidence." It was then that the experience at the lake returned with great meaning. I could see Jenny venturing further and further toward her goal as she frequently stopped just long enough to make sure the raft had not moved, that it was still in the same location, and that it was a safe place she could return to according to her need. It was Jenny who determined when and how often she would return. It was in knowing that the raft was securely tied and would not move that she gained confidence, little by little, until finally she responded to the encouragement of her friends and left the raft, never looking back until she reached her goal.

With this picture in mind, I picked up a pencil and began to explain as I drew. "Just suppose this were a raft, Mrs. Olsen," I said, though I must admit it hardly looked like one, "and that this is a huge rock some distance away in the lake." I recalled in detail my day at the lake, while Mrs. Olsen listened intently, making little response until I finished. She seemed to look past me as though she were still seeing it all. Thoughtfully, she said, "Linda needs a safe place, a raft that won't move. It's Linda who needs to move out, not her father and I. We've been moving the raft away from Linda, instead of allowing Linda to leave the raft with the confidence that she can return at any time." The conference was brief, and Mrs. Olsen left expressing thanks.

During the next few weeks, I watched Linda carefully as she faced her many challenges. Hoping she might gradually venture away from her safe place, I resolved to be a raft for her where she could return as needed and receive reinforcement.

About six weeks later I was on playground duty again, standing alone just around the corner of the building out of the wind. I could hear the clang of the tetherball chains as they hit the metal poles where the children stood waiting in line for their turn. It was Linda's turn next. Just before leaving her place in line, she turned to look in my direction. I waved at her, and, with a big smile, she eagerly stepped up and took her turn. Hitting the ball on the first try, she got the chain wrapped around the pole three times before her opponent could alter its direction. She kept her eye on the ball, never looking back. I realized then that Linda's safe place was expanding to encompass the entire playground and hopefully beyond.

About two weeks later, the school secretary delivered a note to my room. "Please call Mrs. Olsen at your convenience. It is not urgent." In spite of the indication of no urgency, I was anxious to talk to Mrs. Olsen so I returned her call immediately.

"I hope I didn't interrupt you, Mrs. Kapp," she said, "but I thought you'd be interested to know that this morning at the breakfast table, Linda casually announced, 'Becky,'—who is her friend, as you know—'has moved her bedroom downstairs, where she has lots of room. Can I move my bedroom downstairs in Sandra's room, just while she's away at school?' Mrs. Kapp, you may not realize what this means to us, but we had made this suggestion several months ago. At that time it was so frightening to Linda that she burst into tears, saying she'd be too scared; and now this morning, she is asking to move her things downstairs. I just wanted to call and say thanks for helping me to see the importance of encouraging her to move away from me, rather than me moving away from her. Actually, it seems like we're even closer in our relationship than we were before, in spite of the fact that she wants to be in Sandra's room. I suspect that maybe the first night or two, she will come upstairs before morning, and if she does you can be sure I'll be here, not to tell her to go back down, as I would have done some weeks ago, but rather to let her feel the security of the raft until she's ready to venture forth again."

As I returned to my classroom, I reflected on this experience. I wondered about other children who might feel anxious about the dependability of their safe place. It's true: a place is only safe if it is dependable, if it is secure, if it is steady. It might be an old water-soaked raft, a teacher, or a parent, but if it is to be a safe place, it must be always there and always be dependable.

There's a Bright Side

Jeffery's name was sixth from the bottom on the list of students assigned to be in my class during the fourth grade. On his permanent record was the notation, "Unable to master reading skills." Something about the finality reflected in the heaviness of the ink and the width of the letters made me resist that accusation and modify it in my mind to read "has not *yet* mastered reading skills." Right then I determined that if this boy were willing, the entry for the current year would read differently.

Jeffery was happy and confident on the playground. He was good competition for any of the boys on the softball field, and they would often tag around him, which sort of made up for how he must have felt in class. Frequently he would be out of school for two or three days at a time, and on his return he would tell about going with his dad in the truck. He would explain about gas mileage, depreciation, and highway construction with greater ease than he could read a first-grade primer. It was just in school through repeated failure experiences that he assumed he was dumb. One day, in response to my anxious concern and determination to help him, he resisted by simply explaining in a matter-of-fact tone that he was dumb. I placed both hands firmly on his shoulders and looked him squarely in the eyes. While giving him a good shake, I explained that such a comment would not be tolerated in our room. With more surprise than concern, he looked wide-eyed and maybe even a little hopeful.

From that day on, we began studying word lists together: call, ball, tall, hall; can, man, tan, fan, pan; and on and on. Ever so slowly, he began coming up with the right responses. To protect him from the failure and embarrassment among his friends that he had experienced so often, I made a habit of always asking a question first of a student who could give the right answer; then, rephrasing the question so as not to be too obvious, I would direct the next question, requiring the very same answer, to Jeffery. He learned to be a good listener and began to feel the rewards of giving right answers. Gradually the other students began to discover that even in the classroom, he wasn't dumb after all.

Fall turned to winter, and weeks of drilling during recess and early mornings slipped behind us. The risk involved in giving a wrong answer faded away. Even the tenseness that I often felt as I strained to assist him, as though that might be of any help, no longer existed. Our word games became fun. Day by day, Jeffery's willingness to put in extra time was paying off. Together we were making progress and enjoying our shared accomplishments.

It was during social studies that the real test came. I had just asked Matt what part the mountain men had played in the settling of Utah, and he explained that Jim Bridger, for one, had found the Great Salt Lake and thought it was the Pacific Ocean because it was so salty. Wanting to involve Jeffery in the discussion, I carefully phrased a question for him so that again he might have a success experience. He appeared to be listening, so I asked, "Jeffery, what was the one thing Jim Bridger did?"

Jeffery looked straight ahead and didn't respond. To avoid weakening his emerging confidence, I quickly called on someone else and got the answer. "He thought he found the Pacific Ocean." Once again I returned to Jeffery. "Instead of the Pacific Ocean, what did he find, Jeffery?" Jeffery refused to respond. It seemed at that moment that all my time, my sacrifice, my determination had been in vain. It seemed to me that this young man owed me something for all my effort. Should I care if he didn't? If he was not willing at least to try, I was ready to give up. I repeated the question and waited with increased insistence. His eyes met mine. I said nothing. It seemed that the entire class was hanging on this moment. Would Jeffery answer? What would the teacher do if he didn't?

Having determined to take a firm stand and insist that the child share some responsibility, I chose not to let him off as I would otherwise have done. "Jeffery, I don't care if your answer is wrong," I said, "but I want a response." I continued to increase the pressure by not taking my eyes from him. As I watched him, his eyes appeared to begin to water, and I wasn't sure if it was my imagination, but his cheeks seemed to puff up. With some anxiety, I moved closer to him. With a feeling of frantic concern, I noticed red seeping from the corners of his mouth. My mind flooded with anxious thoughts. I'd never heard of a teacher's wrath causing a child to bleed from the mouth. Suddenly I felt that I was being held in judgment before the entire class and the whole world for abusing a child.

Jeffery, trying now to cover his mouth with the sleeve of his shirt, ran from his desk to the sink in the back of the room. Red drops were falling on the floor as he went. A hush fell over the room as Timmy and Mark joined him at the sink to witness what was taking place. I rushed back to help, and just as I put my arm around his shoulder and tried with the other hand to hold his head over the sink, which was spotted with large red drops, he stood straight up and, with his hand to his mouth, removed two small pieces of metal. Instantly I recognized them as the small cartridge of a red ballpoint pen that had separated in the middle, releasing the entire contents in his mouth. He looked at me; I looked at him; and the entire class watched us both in silence. Everyone waited, wondering what would the teacher do now.

In that second, Timmy, who sometimes disrupted class because of his spontaneous, happy spirit, sized up the whole situation and, with the wisdom of a sage, began to laugh! It was contagious. John responded the same way, then Carol and Susan, and finally the teacher gained enough composure to join in the laughter. With the humorous response from Timmy and the help of the class, Jeffery was recognized by all the students as having played a real joke on the teacher, and we all laughed together.

Laughter must be a common experience in a classroom, so that when it is needed, the children will be quickly responsive. It may preserve a relationship between a teacher and a child that has been months in the making, a relationship that might otherwise be greatly weakened, if not destroyed.

By the end of the year, with the help of many of his friends who diligently worked with him, Jeffery was reading, and we all shared in his success. Occasionally after that when we would be sharing happy times and reminiscing, someone would say, "Remember the day Mrs. Kapp wanted Jeffery to answer a question, and he wouldn't?" Then we'd all laugh together, and quietly I would think to myself, every class needs a Timmy to laugh and ease the strain for everyone. I would remember the lines by Rolfe, the great Shakespearean scholar: "He must be a fool who cannot at times play the fool, and he that does not enjoy nonsense must be lacking in sense."

A Gift of Understanding

Some children always seem to get the teacher's attention first, either by waving their arms, snapping their fingers, or speaking out. Others wait patiently with their hands held high for so long that sometimes the other arm is used as a brace—reaching across, grabbing a hold at the elbow, and resting the support arm on the top of the head. A solution to this awkward position and waste of time was easily resolved by a suggestion from Kim: From that day on, every child who needed help had a fair chance as he would simply add his name to the bottom of the list lying on the teacher's desk.

Kerry's turn was next. Even with the many problems students have with long division, he hadn't had to wait very long for his turn with the teacher. As prescribed, Kerry's paper had been carefully folded once, and then again and again, until when the paper was unfolded, small squares about two inches by three inches were measured off across the entire page. A single problem had been copied very carefully in each square, and the first six had been answered. Kerry's desk was as neat as his paper. His sensitivity to tidiness carried over in his person. His hair was always in place and even his freckles seemed to be sprinkled in an orderly fashion across the bridge of his nose and on his cheeks.

Kneeling on one knee by his desk so I could look him in the eye, I asked in a quiet voice, "How can I help you, Kerry?"

"I don't get it," he said, pointing to problem number seven in the textbook. He had copied it accurately on his paper, but the answer was missing. He waited for help.

Being anxious to assist, I jumped right in as I thought a good teacher would. "Let me show you, Kerry," I said, with a desire to be cooperative and supportive. "How many times does nine go into sixty-eight?" I asked, wanting to involve him in the solution.

"Seven times," came his quick response; and just as quickly I recorded a seven in the proper space on his paper and continued on.

"And how many times does nine go into fifty-six?" I waited, but there was no response. I repeated the question. Just then I noticed the delicate skin on his neck around his ears. It appeared a little blotchy. A teacher must watch for even the slightest clues if she is to fully understand a child's feelings and strengthen his environment so maximum learning can take place. I had taken great pride in my ability to do this because of my concern for each student. To reassure Kerry, I emphasized that not knowing the answer was of little concern because this was a time for learning. This comment seemed to make no difference, so to reassure him of my willingness to help, I quickly finished problem seven and went on to the next problem.

By now his head was lowered, and I couldn't see his eyes, but when a tear dropped on the page and quickly spread out on it, I was concerned. In one fleeting second I tried to recall all I had learned about teaching methods and understanding children, and nothing like this was in any of the books I had studied.

Deeply concerned, I got up from my kneeling position and looked down at the child bent over his paper. It was only then that I saw the mistake—the very obvious mistake. Kneeling again, I looked at Kerry as I pointed to the obtrusive numbers from a careless red marking pencil, which at that moment seemed to cover the entire page. "Did I ruin your paper?" I asked. Without a sound, but with tears filling his eyes and his lips tightly closed, he nodded his head.

In that moment, I sensed the realization that it was the teacher, not the child, who was on trial. No, I didn't recall reading about a situation like this in the books, but it was clear to me now that I had jumped in too quickly, too eagerly, and had been more concerned with the child's understanding the problem than with my understanding the child. Now the teacher faced the challenge and opportunity to restore and set aright the situation, if possible.

Could a ruined paper be repaired?

Could a troubled child be consoled?

Could a thoughtless teacher be redeemed?

I looked at the definite crease through the carefully folded paper around the two squares marred by the red pencil. "I have an idea, Kerry," I said with a tone of confidence, which brought a quick look of hope to his wide-open, trusting eyes. "We can take the scissors and cut along these lines," I explained as I traced around the entire spoiled area with my finger.

He watched with some concern as I carefully cut along the folded line until the marked portion was almost cut out. With the last snip of the scissors, the red-marked rectangle, about four inches by six inches, fell to the desk and was separated from its origin. Immediately the situation looked more hopeful.

"Kerry," I explained, "we can get a piece of paper and tape it on the back with masking tape." With just a slight look of questioning on his part, I quickly pointed out that the tape would be on the back and wouldn't show. With that, the corners of his mouth turned up slightly, and an expression of "let's try it" was easily read.

With the repairs made and the two questions (including the answers) recopied onto the carefully mended paper, Kerry paused only a moment as if to take stock of the accomplishments made. Then, with a gesture of confidence, he continued on immediately as if to make up for lost time.

Kerry learned quickly the simple process for long division, but it took the teacher considerably longer to learn a more valuable lesson in awareness and understanding.

It's an Emergency

Ernest hardly ever had much to say. From the first day of class, when his mother had brought him to the door and tried to encourage him by giving him a gentle push on the back, he had remained quiet and alone. During recess, as the boys chose sides for their games, I felt concern, for Ernest was always chosen last or not at all.

Ernest chose to sit near the back of the room, and he seldom raised his hand or volunteered to take part even in the jobs such as cleaning the chalk brushes, which always brought a chorus of volunteers from all the others. If he had ever indicated any such interest, I'm sure he'd have had the job immediately. I so wanted him to be involved and enjoy school. The thought of any child spending seven hours a day, day after day, feeling left out or unimportant was a burden I did not want to shoulder.

Near the end of class one day while the children were all busy with various assignments, I found myself wandering up and down the aisles with a half-smile, pleased at their industry. As I brushed past Ernest's desk, I caught only the last word of his comment and quickly turned back to hear more.

With his head up, he said, "Can I give a report on fish?"

My first thought was, *Fish?* How does that tie into anything we're doing? Excited about his willingness to participate, however, I enthusiastically assured him that he could give his report, and then asked if I could help him in any way. His response was a respectful but brief "No." "When would you like to give the report?" He replied, "I'll let you know."

Almost two months had passed since the first day of school, and the growth and progress of some students was much more visible than that of others, but I had learned that often the greatest achievements are made in the privacy of one's own self and sometimes are not evident until much later.

We had a rule in our class, agreed upon by teacher and students alike, that during reading time while the teacher worked with six or eight students around the table in the back of the room, the rest of the children were to work quietly on their own or with prearranged help from other students. They were not to interrupt the reading group unless, of course, it was an emergency. In the case of an emergency, the child interrupting would have to make that determination and we would all respect his judgment in the matter.

The books had been distributed in the reading group and the assignments received. Mark had just begun to introduce the next story, "The Great Canadian Goose," and had located the Hudson Bay area on the map.

I was sitting in a position that enabled me to observe the entire class while participating in the reading group. I noticed Ernest had turned to look out
the door. He waited a moment, then came quietly to
my side and whispered, "I want to give my report
now."

Taken somewhat by surprise, I looked at him
and said, "Now, Ernie?"

He dropped his head and quietly said, "It's an
emergency."

Considering the other students' involvement, I
wondered about Ernie's judgment and the possibility
of delaying him just twenty minutes until we were
finished. In that split second, I also wondered about
the courage it must have taken Ernie, of all people,
to make the judgment that might be considered an
emergency and to come and interrupt the reading
group.

I simply repeated his declaration, "It's an
emergency?" and he nodded his head vigorously.

By now the members of the reading group were
wondering about this interruption. I calmly announced that we would all turn our books over and
return to our seats; we had an emergency, and Ernest
was going to give his report. While the students
surely must have questioned the appropriateness of
Ernie's judgment, their response was to follow the
example of the teacher. With the dignity and importance this young child deserved, I went to the
front of the room and instructed the class that there
was an emergency that required a change in our
schedule. I requested that the desks be cleared off so

full attention could be given, and then announced that Ernie would be presenting a special report on fish.

Many of the students looked at each other with expressions of surprise, but no one hesitated in carrying out the instructions.

I took my place by the bookcase at the side of the room as Ernest walked to the front and, with a stronger voice than I had ever heard from him, announced, "My report is on fish." At that moment he motioned toward the door, and in came his older brother carrying a huge frozen salmon. Ernie met him halfway, took the salmon, and returned to the front of the class as his brother left.

By now all eyes were on him as he held in both arms against his chest what turned out to be a thirty-six-inch salmon. From where I stood the huge eyes of the frozen salmon looked much like the wide eyes of many of the students.

Ernie told of how he and his father had gone fishing on the Columbia River during the summer, and how his mother had promised him and his brother that the day she took it out of the freezer, they could take it to school. He then went into great detail about how salmon climb the ladders, go out to the ocean, and return again to lay their eggs. Finally, with increased enthusiasm, he told how he and his dad caught this great fish.

By now the excitement in the room was so high that Ernie began talking faster and faster. As he did so, the grip of his arms around the fish, which had now begun to thaw, became increasingly tighter, causing the salmon to lunge upward. Marty spoke out in excitement, saying she'd never seen a live fish like that before! Ernie regained control and, hand over hand, brought the slippery fish back into position against his chest. His shirt was now wet and a bit scaly and slightly smelly.

In that one-half hour Ernie held captive twenty-eight students and one teacher as he told his story of courage, valor, and victory. After many questions from students now sitting on their feet in their seats to improve their view, Ernie gave a little nod, indicating the performance was over. He left the platform like a hero, and all eyes followed him as he carried the subject of his victory to his brother, who was waiting in the hall. By the end of the day, the front of Ernie's shirt was stiff, the smell in the room was strong, and the unnumbered victories of that experience were yet to be measured.

From that day on, it was different for Ernie. The students thought if he could fish, he could do anything else. Instead of being last, he was now chosen first. Instead of sitting alone, he was the center of attention and everyone wanted to sit by him. He was still Ernie, but in his own quiet way, he began to unfold like a butterfly emerging from a cocoon.

At the close of that day when all the students were gone, and with the strong smell of fish mingled with chalk dust lingering in the room, I sat alone at my desk and almost fearfully reflected on what might have been. Just suppose I had asked Ernie to wait until after reading group to attend to his emergency, or suppose we had no emergency policy in our class. Had that been the case, I'm sure he would never have had the courage to persist or even explain. In my mind's eye, I could see him returning quietly to his seat, his head dropped in its usual way, with the report never given. Thinking of Ernie, I offered a quiet prayer that I might be as successful in all my fishing as he was in his.

"And he saith unto them, Follow me, and I will make you fishers of men. And they straightway left their nets, and followed him." (Matthew 4:19-20.)

More Than Was Expected

In Mrs. Watson's second grade class every student knew his place and knew exactly what was expected of him. Every Monday between ten and eleven o'clock it was story time, followed by show-and-tell on Tuesday, physical education on Wednesday, music on Thursday, and always art on Friday.

It was expected that on Friday at ten o'clock each child would go to the closet, find his own paint shirt, which in most cases had formerly belonged to a father or brother, and put it on, usually backwards. The children would then help each other by buttoning at least the first two buttons of the shirt before the owners would impatiently move forward, at which time it was someone else's turn to be buttoned up.

Each child would then go to the newspaper drawer stacked with carefully folded newspapers, pick one sheet folded in half, and return to his desk. After placing their papers squarely on the table in front of them, the students would wait patiently for Mrs. Watson to give further instructions.

Mrs. Watson would measure just the right amount of poster paint, glue, or whatever was to be used, as she moved up and down each row in order. This procedure was followed by instructions that always ended with, "Be careful not to waste, don't spill, and save all of the extra scraps of paper to be put in the scrap-paper drawer."

Miss Rowery was the new student teacher, and it was expected that she would follow the same routine that had been painstakingly developed with the children over several months. By 10:10 on Friday morning every child sat in his place, paint shirt on, with a sheet of newspaper folded in half in front of him. In addition to the paper, everyone had a much-used plastic bowl that bore some evidence through the rainbow of paints dried on the outside of once having been a cottage cheese carton. Beside each bowl was a small plastic spoon. Mrs. Watson, seeing everything was in order and feeling confident that there would be no unexpected situations, planned to leave the room, allowing Miss Rowery to assume the full responsibility of a teacher. The children knew from experience that eleven o'clock would be the time to clean up, and their deportment was predictable.

I was sitting in the back by the sink in the place appointed in this room for the supervising teacher. As Mrs. Watson left the room, closing the door behind her, she smiled with an expression of confidence, even though she would not be returning until sometime after lunch.

To insure a successful art lesson, Miss Rowery had taken time to carefully measure all of the necessary ingredients for the salt dough, except for the water, into twenty-four separate little plastic bags. The children were told to empty the contents of their bags into their bowls and begin to mix the ingredients while she provided the right amount of water for each child.

Immediately I sensed some concern as this capable young teacher recognized a situation she had not anticipated. Her attention was on James, who had just emptied the entire contents from the plastic bag into his bowl, filling it to the very top. Quickly he covered it with both hands as though it might be discovered that he had an unusually large portion and might have to share. Every bag had the same amount of salt and flour and every bowl was the same size, so there was little or no room left for the water.

While the amount of flour and the size of the bowl were the same for each child, there was a vast difference in the responses from the twenty-four individual students. Everyone began talking at once.

"Is this all for me?" was the question of a timid little girl who appeared never to have had a full measure of anything.

The eyes of a little red-headed girl seemed to get larger and larger as she continued to pour the flour far beyond the portion that usually just filled the bottom of the bowl.

One young boy, now sitting on his feet in his chair and looking at the contents of his bowl, expressed his excitement by slapping his chest with both hands and declaring, "I can build a mountain!"

What some of the children viewed as an opportunity became a trap for others, and they sat waiting, bewildered by this unexpected abundance.

Miss Rowery, untroubled by her miscalculation, made a quick observation and considered the alternatives. She could retrieve from each child's bowl a few spoonfuls of flour and remove the challenge of keeping it in the bowl while mixing the water. As I watched her, however, with her chin in her hand while supporting her arm at the elbow with the other arm, it appeared that she might be considering another possibility. The undetermined benefits of this situation might be even more important than the extravagance of using too much salt and flour.

Having made a decision, she came to the rescue of those who did not know what to do. With a happy countenance and a pleasant voice, she said to the class, "I see that your bowls are very full." Then, to avoid the risk of assuming problems where they might not even exist, she made a further observation and requested a response. "With your bowls filled nearly to the top, is this a problem for anyone?"

Billy, defending his right to such abundance, began immediately to explain all the things he could do with it.

Priscilla appeared much less eager. Having carefully filled her bowl, and with both hands in her lap, she had an expression of concern on her face. "But what if I spill it?" was her response.

To that Miss Rowery explained, "You probably will, Priscilla. That's the very reason for the newspaper." With that the child raised one hand and began to stir the water in her too-full bowl.

Mixing the dough became a valuable part of the lesson. With so much extra dough, the children began to explore many options that had not been available to them before. Even those who seemed at first burdened by too much to handle soon discovered that it was only too much if one didn't know what to do with it. They began to expand their ideas to match the challenge.

Leaving my seat in the back of the room, I walked up and down each row and observed the creative work of children. The usual items made from salt-and-flour dough, such as balls, boxes, and bowls, had been replaced by castles, cars, and cupboards, with enough dough left over for extras.

Time passed quickly as ideas became realities in the hands of these little designers. Walking toward Priscilla's desk, I noticed her motion to her friend Kathy and point at the clock as she began putting the loose dough from the paper back into the bowl even though she wasn't finished. As I glanced at the clock, I realized that it was ten to eleven, time to quit creating, according to schedule. It seemed, however, that the others had lost all track of time, as their hands worked quickly to keep pace with their minds.

Can an idea be programmed, scheduled, regulated, and terminated according to schedule? Can a creative thought be set aside before it is really born and then be returned to again next Friday at ten o'clock?

The clock ticked on as the children continued uninterrupted. Those who had completed their works of art ahead of the others were deeply enthralled with a more thorough examination of their accomplishments. It was time for admiring, sharing, discovering, and even bragging.

The ecstasy of one little girl could not be contained by just sharing with her friends. With her prize carefully cupped between both hands and her arms carefully tucked closely against her sides, she seemed to protectively hunch over her piece as she went from one friend to another and then to Miss Rowery. Finally it was my turn to share in the joy of her accomplishment.

With her eyes glued on her work and without looking up, she put her cupped hands forward, displaying a flat rounded shape with various unidentifiable indentations. To my questioning mind, she provided an immediate answer. "Look, Mrs. Kapp. Look at my beautiful, beautiful mother."

She then looked up as if to verify my understanding. As I glanced again at her work of art, I could clearly see two big eyes, curly hair at the top, and an oversized smile that expanded the full width of the face.

Surely she had created a work of art. With enough material and time, she had drawn from the deep reservoir of her inner feelings; and judging from her display of ecstasy mingled with a sense of reverence, she saw what I was not able to see. Yet, in my mind, I knew unquestionably that this work of art was in fact a masterpiece.

It's One of Those Days

It just isn't possible to always be happy and patient, cooperative and good-natured. Some days even ordinary, routine things have a way of being irritating and distracting, and one searching for a reason for such days may find the answer to be simply: "It's just one of those days." They come and they go, and not always with a reasonable explanation.

Children learn quickly to recognize these days, and they also learn to make their special requests "when she's in a good mood." At the beginning of the year, the students and I talked together about these kinds of feelings so we could understand each other better. Occasionally, one of the very perceptive students would inquire, "Is it one of those days?" and if I'd say "Yes," there were usually one or two who seemed to sense some responsibility to assist in making things better. Children learn to be aware of others and their feelings as others relate to them in a sensitive way.

One day Billy had been particularly observant of signals of which I was not aware, although I would have to admit to a feeling of impatience and frustration. It was late in the afternoon and I sat working intensely at my desk, struggling with the burdensome role of judge as I tried to place grades on each child's report card. I had not noticed Billy leave his desk, but when I heard a whisper in my ear, I turned to see a tousle-haired boy with an expression of genuine concern in his eyes.

"Is this the kind of day that makes the teacher want to climb the wall?" he whispered.

I looked into his youthful face and, touched by his sensitivity, I nodded, affirming his speculation. Just his gentle inquiry seemed to ease much of the burden.

Returning to his desk, he passed the word to those closest to him, "Hey, kids, it's one of those days for the teacher."

There is power and strength in unity, and together these youngsters almost immediately changed the feeling in the room. It became unusually quiet, and in the quiet could be sensed concern for one another.

Just as surely as teachers have some of those days, children also have bad days. We often talked together about how we could handle these kinds of days and how we could help each other. Jeff suggested, "If I want something, but if I think you'll say no just because it's a bad day, then I will wait until tomorrow to ask." I agreed that that would probably help. My concern had to do with the teacher's responsibility to be aware and sensitive to the children's feelings when they had one of those days. After discussion, they decided that if a child was being scolded, corrected, or counseled and it was honestly one of those hard-to-take days, then the child could tell the teacher and, if possible, corrective measures might be delayed—but not dismissed. So together we learned respect for each other's bad days while we worked hard in an effort to make them all good.

On a Thursday afternoon in October, after the rest of the students had left, only Jake remained at his desk. By four P.M. he was still sitting there, staring into space, with his workbook open and the work still waiting to be done.

Children must learn responsibility and accountability. They must learn to suffer the consequences of their decisions. Jake had made a choice when he had failed to do his lessons during the day. He knew well in advance he would need to remain after school, and so there he sat. I was prepared to wait it out with him, or so I thought. The room was silent except for the sound of the custodian, whose dust broom knocked rhythmically against the tile under the coat racks in the hall.

I looked up when I heard voices coming from the hall.

"You ask her," said one, and then a quiet response, "No, you." Even without an explanation, the problem was clear when I saw Jeff and David standing in the hall with their softball mitts dangling from their hands.

As I approached the door, their concern for who was to be spokesman became of little consequence as they both began to explain, "Mrs. Kapp, you've got

to let him go. We have a Little League practice and
Jake is our pitch." Then David, hitting his fist into
the cup of his well-worn mitt, announced, "You've
just gotta, Mrs. Kapp."

I don't know if it was the tone of his voice or the
look in his eye, but his penetrating gaze caused me to
glance toward Jeff for some relief, only to feel the
same intensity in Jeff's countenance. Frequently
pleas from students are accompanied with coaxing
and sometimes whining. Had that been the case this
time, I'm sure I could have stood my ground, but it
was the silence, the unbroken silence of these two
defenders, that demanded consideration.

Without a word, I turned to see Jake still sitting
in his desk like a defendant awaiting a verdict.
"Okay, boys," I said, "come in. Let's talk about it
and we'll see what can be done."

After what must have seemed to the boys like a
lengthy discourse on mercy and justice, I finally
asked for their recommendation. Jake was the first
to speak up. "If I promise to do my work before I
come in the morning, would that be justice?" Before
I could respond, Jeff seemed to wrap it all up by adding, "And you could let him go and that would be
mercy."

The principles seemed correct, if they were fully
understood, and to insure that complete understanding, I added what must have sounded like the
second verse to a song they'd already heard. "There
must be no misunderstanding," I began, and Jake
interrupted with "Promise, Mrs. Kapp, I promise."

The verdict was decided, the challengers had

won, and they rushed out together with full confidence in another victory ahead on the ball field.

The next morning I stood at the door in my usual place to acknowledge each child if only with a glance, a smile, or an arm around the shoulder of one who, judging by his or her countenance, might have left a troubled home.

I was anticipating a report from Jake, first about the game, of course, and then about the homework. Out of the corner of my eye I caught sight of him in the hall. Several students arrived at the door at the same time, and he seemed to be waiting to crowd through without being noticed.

The problem was obvious and was confirmed as I said, "Jake?" He turned his head away. This was a private matter and should not involve the whole class. I must get the day started for the others, free of trouble or concern, and then come back to the problem at the proper time.

The tension grew. I glanced at Jake frequently while he sat staring at his desk. With the class now busy at their work, I walked toward the back of the room past Jake's desk and quietly said, "Jake, could I see you, please?"

It wasn't the unfinished homework that gave me greatest concern, but the need for a lesson in responsibility, accountability, and trust.

Jake got up from his desk and followed me back to the reading table, where we sat across from each other. The interrogation began.

"You don't have your lessons done," I said in a statement more of fact than of inquiry.

"No."

"Did you understand the agreement and commitment?"

He dropped his eyes and in a quiet voice whispered, "Yes."

And then the teacher, having verified the situation, was ready to exert the necessary authoritative measures and defend justice at all cost. In a quiet but stern voice, I began to unload all my disappointment in a boy who couldn't be trusted.

"Just what does your word mean?" I asked in less than a gentle tone.

With his head down, he muffled under his breath, "Mrs. Kapp?"

"Yes?" I said, still waiting for the answer.

"It's one of those days."

I was not prepared for that answer. *Sure it is,* I thought. *Who do you think you're kidding, young man?*

There was silence, neither the student nor the teacher knowing what to do. Then, as if to break the silence, or at least verify the message, he looked up. Something in his expression made it immediately a matter to be dealt with by the heart and spirit rather than by the mind and logic.

"Do you want to talk about it?" I asked in a gentle tone. Without a word, he just shook his head.

There was no way of knowing just what was going on inside the lad, but it was obviously a matter of great concern as he sat slumped over in his chair. A teacher can't always remove the problem and may not even help lift the load, but a teacher who really cares can avoid adding additional burdens to young shoulders often weighted down unmercifully by out-side pressures. As I placed my hand gently on his shoulder, he seemed to sense my concern. We sat together in silence, allowing just enough time for a teacher to place the welfare of a boy before the urgency to enforce rules and justice.

No longer able to carry the load, he looked up. Tears filled his eyes, then began flowing down his young, suntanned face. With no attempt to hide the tears, he poured out his story, his young shoulders shaking as he released all the anguish he could no longer contain.

"Mrs. Kapp," he said, "last night my mom told me that her and Dad are getting a divorce. My dad's gone to California and isn't coming back, and I'm supposed to stay with my mom." Then his eyes closed as he laid his head across his arm on the table and sobbed, "And I love my dad."

We sat in silence. Then, after a moment, Jake raised his head, wiped his face with the sleeve of his wrinkled shirt, and looked at me. "Jake," I whispered, "is there anything I can do to help you?"

He shook his head. Then, picking up his book, he said, "Can you give me another chance for my homework?"

At a time when there seemed so little a teacher could do to lift the burden, it was clear there was a way to avoid adding to it.

"Yes, Jake, I can give you another chance," I said. But my most immediate concern was my own chance—my chance, in some way, to possibly follow the example of the great Master Teacher.

"Jake," I said, "bring your book and come with me."

Over by the window where the early morning sun was shining on the old piece of carpet donated by one of the parents to make a special spot in our room, we sat together. Referring only briefly to the workbook to take care of Jake's need to fulfill his sense of responsibility, we talked through many problems. I mostly listened, asking only enough questions to reassure him of my genuine concern.

Finally the recess bell rang. As if responding to a fire alarm, the students rushed from their desks to pick up their mitts, bats, jump ropes, or whatever.

Bounding toward the door ahead of the rest, Jeff turned, looked at Jake, and waited. "Are you coming, Jake?" he called.

I looked at Jake, the trace of a smile on his tear-stained face.

"I think they need you," I said.

As he got up to leave, he asked, "Do you think you could come out and watch us play?"

At that moment it seemed like the most important thing I might do all day.

I did watch, and on that occasion I saw a courageous young boy, encouraged by the support of his friends, struggle with considerable risk and a heavy burden and make it from one base to the next clear around the ball diamond. From where I was standing I could see that determined look in his eyes as he bit his lower lip. Running at full speed he caused the dust to fly as he slid in, making a home run for his team, even though it was one of those days.

Different but Not Dumb

"I'm dumb," Marty would whisper half under her breath as I would bend down to help her with her work.

It was true—Marty did have some difficulties in school and, as her teacher, I was anxious to help her, but it seemed that her attitude about herself was more of a problem than her actual lack of ability. She just thought she was "dumb," and try as I would, there seemed to be no way of changing her mind.

On back-to-school night, after all the other parents had left the room, Marty's father remained. He looked somewhat oversized as he got up from his daughter's desk where he'd been sitting during the presentation. In his hand he held a small card. Like all the other children, Marty had prepared a sample of her work for her parents. Hers was made of light blue construction paper trimmed artistically with delicate paper cuttings of the most intricate design. I watched her father as he carefully opened the card, read again the brief but sensitive message inside, and then spoke with compassion and love. "She may be different," he said, dropping his eyes to look again at the card, "but she isn't dumb," he added with a tone of assurance.

His voice and the manner in which he handled the card gave me reason to believe he had much more to say. Pointing to a larger chair by the table, I suggested that he have a seat. I was anxious to better understand what Marty's father knew so that I might share in that same confidence. He leaned forward, rested his elbows on the table, and began to speak of Marty not so much by way of explanation, justification, or even expectation, but out of concern that I understand.

"Marty," he explained, "has missed a lot of school over the past years because of illness, and as a result, she hasn't done as well as her older brothers and sisters. She has it so strongly implanted in her mind that she often even says she is dumb." Repeating his earlier statement as if to make sure I understood, he said, "It's true, she is different." Then, pausing a moment to be assured he had my full attention, he continued, "but she isn't dumb."

When someone, especially a parent, has confidence in a child, and that confidence is expressed consistently, the child's ability seems almost magically commensurate with the expressed confidence. I thought of Marty's great advantage in having a father who knew she wasn't dumb. I thought also of the child in the first grade down the hall who frequently remained after school and, in response to her teacher's inquiry as to why she didn't go home, said, "But Mrs. Page, you're the only one that knows I'm smart."

For Marty, it was her father who understood something of her great potential and was speaking in her behalf. When he got up to leave, he expressed appreciation for my time, and I followed him to the door, an advocate for his little girl.

Returning to the classroom, I looked at Marty's desk, neat and tidy, everything in place. *Yes, Marty, I thought, I do understand. You are different, just like every other student in this classroom; but you, like they, are not dumb, and somehow, some way you must find that out.* I sat and pondered, *How can this happen? There must be some way.*

My sister Sharon, who was also a teacher, seemed to have an unending supply of good ideas and had just related to me an interesting experiment she had tried with great success in her class. While the objective of her lesson was quite different, the same experiment might well serve to teach another lesson. She was teaching economics, division of labor, and specialization. Could the same approach that she used teach an even more important lesson? It was worth a try.

The next morning came and so did the children. The regular preliminaries were followed by reports from the children to me about what their moms and dads had said about back-to-school night, then a question-and-answer session. (They wanted to know what their moms and dads had said to me about them.) Finally the day was off to a good start—that is, until Brent noticed an unusually long list of assignments on the chalkboard. Instead of just one page of arithmetic, there were two. The same with

spelling and English. In addition to the regular
assignments for Wednesday, there were assignments
in dictionary skills that were usually delayed until
Friday. Added to all of that was an assignment for
one piece of original art.

Immediately the anxiety level was evident.
Sheila, a self-appointed spokesman for the class, attempted to come to the defense of all of the students
and protect everyone from such injustice.

To their many questions I responded, "Yes, you
are expected to do all of the assignments before you
leave tonight. Yes, they must be turned in by the
end of the day." Then, to establish some kind of
control, I extended both hands with palms down
and motioned up and down as if to keep the lid on
the boiling pot. "Quiet down and let me explain," I
said.

They seemed willing to listen to any explanation
for such seeming inconsideration and so I began.
"We need to discover the great resources that we
have in our classroom, like the resources we have in
our community, and how dependent we are on each
other."

I could tell by the look on Sheila's face that I
hadn't yet said anything to alleviate her concern for
the assignments, but with a smile I continued. "We
cannot all do the same things equally well, and even
if we could, it might not be the best way." To make
the point, I asked Tiffany, whose father was a
hairdresser, if he had built their house. She said she
didn't know who had built it, but she was sure it
hadn't been her dad. Then I asked whose father was

a builder, and Christy told about all the houses her dad had built. Before long, everyone had joined in the discussion and together we discovered the need for every dad's service and how dependent we all are on each other.

With that discussion as a base, I suggested to the students that today we would take advantage of the resources in our classroom and each one could go to whomever they wished to get their work done—but it had to be a good job and they had to do something in return. Again the questions came, but with much more enthusiasm this time.

"You mean it's okay if I get Dave to do my arithmetic?" asked Linda, and I nodded approval.

"And can Christy do my spelling?" inquired Chad.

Then Timmy, who seemed to be the least artistic, spoke loud enough for all to hear, "And is it okay if Marty does my artwork?"

Again I nodded, and looked out of the corner of my eye to see a surprised look on Marty's face. "You're getting the idea," I said. "It's called a division of labor, and we will use the expertise of everyone."

But now my only concern was for the noise in the classroom. How little noise could be made and still allow all to be talking at once? So we had a trial run. On the first try, it was much too noisy. We tried again and again. On the third try, everyone had discovered that just a little louder than a whisper made it all right for everyone to talk at once, and so they began.

Without any discussion, it seemed every child knew which five or six students were the most able in math, and had lined up to arrange for those services; the same for spelling and each of the other subjects. The excitement came after the experts had completed their own assignments and then had only to copy the answers onto six or eight other papers for their friends. Instead of taking all day as they had supposed, by lunchtime almost everyone was reporting with great excitement that all of their work was completed.

The one assignment that was taking longer than all the rest was the piece of original art. It was not so easily copied as math, spelling, or English, but without any question it was the most rewarding, the most successful, and the most important work of the day. Marty had a line of several students standing around her desk waiting their turn for her to help each one assemble the pattern she had cut for a beautiful collage of colors, textures, and designs.

I walked over to observe this diligent little expert sitting at the table with glue, paper, and scissors, and surrounded by students on every side. Her hands were busily arranging a special design for Becky, who was next in line. With a big smile Marty glanced up and, as if she could contain the joy of her discovery not a moment longer, blurted out, "I'm not dumb after all!"

I turned my head quickly, and casually walked over to my desk to avoid having to make an explanation to some curious student about "Why have you got tears in your eyes, Mrs. Kapp?"

The following day began with a long explanation of why it wasn't all right to always do our work that way, since it takes less time and is better work. A lot more time was spent talking about the many talents, gifts, and abilities that were represented in our class, and what a serious loss it would be if even one were missing. Yesterday's work had been put away and almost forgotten, except for the artwork, which was artistically arranged on the front bulletin board for everyone to enjoy.

As the weeks slipped by, it seemed that those gifts discovered in one area lent strength to other areas so that with the students' increased confidence, more and more discoveries were made and lessons learned. Surely the greatest and most important lesson, not only for Marty, but for every child in the class, had been the discovery that we are all different, but not dumb.

Tough Love

We sat alone together in the principal's office. Jan wore one of the only two dresses she had worn all semester. Her hands were clenched together in her lap and her eyes were fixed on the floor. I felt, as usual, that my well-intended words of counsel for her were heard only by me; and just as before, the concerns for her progress and success seemed not to be shouldered by her, but to rest on my shoulders alone, and they weighed heavily.

Jan was a student of mine who had set a goal some years ago to attend the university. According to her own report, she had developed an obsession to attend college, and on her own had worked out a plan to achieve her goal. For two long summers, she had picked potatoes and cucumbers and berries while the scorching sun beat down relentlessly. It was her commitment and determination that had carried her through the long, hot, tiresome days of hard work.

This was her third year in college, and it was now just three weeks until the end of the semester when student teaching would be completed; at least that was the way the schedule read. Everyone assumed that when January 14 arrived, another hurdle would be crossed and student teaching would be a thing of the past—that was, except for Jan, or so it appeared.

We sat together in silence as she fidgeted with a piece of chalk, turning it over and over again in her hands. This, I thought, would be my last attempt to get through to her. Not that there was time to salvage a seemingly wasted semester, but maybe consideration of her future was also part of my responsibility.

Can a person fail alone?

Is it not the shared responsibility of all who could have helped if someone falls short of his goal?

Is the blame or burden ever really carried alone?

Who must be accountable, and where had Jan or I, or both of us together, mismanaged this portion of her life, which also included mine?

Knowing of her sacrifice and determination to attend college, it had seemed unnecessary and even inappropriate for me to push her too hard. I thought of how I had visited her class each week to observe her teaching. After she finished, we would talk about the need for better preparation as we reviewed her careless lesson plans. Each week as I left her class we felt good about each other, but not so good about her teaching; and I would think, surely next week will be better.

With these thoughts flooding my mind, I searched for the answer. "Jan," I said, "what has happened?" She looked up for just a moment, her eyes intense, as if she seemed to realize for the first time my concern. I continued, "You didn't pick potatoes and cucumbers in the hot Idaho sun for two long summers without a definite goal in your mind. You paid the price to get to college, but after you got here, was there no longer a goal? Had your dream ended? Had you no thoughts of the next step and the next, and the next? Can you pay that much to enter the race and stop on the first lap? How can you so consistently disregard the need to even try after the self-discipline required to pick those potatoes from sunup to sundown?"

I heard the intensity mounting in my voice, though the tone remained low. "Jan," I said, as if to shift the full burden of responsibility, "this is your load. What are you going to do about it?"

She sat in silence and I waited, resisting the temptation to jump in to ease her discomfort. Finally, after what seemed like hours, she looked up. Her countenance revealed not the slightest sign of resentment or bitterness, but in a tone of deep reflection, she voiced her feelings. "If you had only talked to me in the beginning like you are talking to me now, I think I could have made it." Again I felt the weight, this time magnified manyfold, as it was my time for reflection.

Encouragement, kindness, and understanding are signs of love, but at times maybe there is another kind of love even more important. It's tough love: the love that allows a coach to call the shots with clarity, even the tough calls, and to do it in the heat of the race, not back in the locker room after the final bell. Could this race be extended? I anxiously asked. It must be. Jan must have another chance to be coached by tough love. She had not been tempered by ease and comfort in the past.

It was difficult explaining to the administration of the university that well-established policies must be modified to extend the race and provide another chance for this student. It was difficult to defend the fact that I knew it would be different next time. I acknowledged with greater insight than ever before that it couldn't be just my determination—that in fact it was the student's responsibility and not mine. In my defense, I came to realize it was a plea for my second chance as much as Jan's that I petitioned.

The request was granted, and during the following semester, we worked together with tough love. She now shouldered the responsibility for her progress and became accountable. I avoided the temptation to help carry her load while I tried more diligently than ever before to carry my own. I identified levels of expectations and required regular accountability from her. I helped her evaluate her own progress in measured portions. We learned together that semester, and finished the race before the final bell.

I relived this entire painful, yet beautiful, experience the other evening as my sister Sharon related to me a conversation she had had with her little daughter Shelly. Shelly had been practicing her piano lesson for some time, and each time she reached the last measure of the third line, her fingers stumbled across the keys. Finally, in exasperation, with both hands falling onto the keyboard, she exclaimed, "Mom, what shall I do?"

Her mother might have suggested resting for awhile, bypassing that difficult measure, or she might even have played it for her, which she could have done with great ease, even expertise. But she didn't.

"Shelly," she said, with a hand on her shoulder, "why don't you try it five more times." To this, Shelly resisted. "Oh, Mom, not five." And allowing Shelly to assume the full responsibility, her mother suggested, "Then you decide."

Even at that tender age, Shelly experienced the responsibility her mother was allowing her to shoulder, but as would be expected, she had a countersuggestion to avoid making the decision alone. "No, Mom," she said, "you decide, but don't choose five." Growth comes by carrying the load, and tough love from a parent or teacher helps us keep our expectations in balance with our effort.

Some weeks later Shelly was again preparing for her piano lesson. Mrs. Nelson, her teacher, was one who kept high levels of expectation and did not accept excuses for mediocre preparation. The commitment that was made in the very beginning—to learn to play and to play well—was reinforced each week, and a poorly prepared lesson would cause considerable concern, especially since Shelly dearly loved her teacher and didn't want to disappoint her.

The past week had been unusually busy with family activities and other interruptions, and her hours of practicing had been neglected, but Shelly had learned that excuses were not solutions. She had a better idea. "Mom," she asked, "could you pick me up from school in time for me to come home before going to my piano lesson?'' Not being aware of Shelly's plans, her mother said, "I'll bring your lesson books with me, and we can go directly to Mrs. Nelson's from school." Shelly quickly explained, "No, Mom, I need to come home first. I would like to have a little prayer before I go for my lesson." Her mother must have smiled inside, sensing the seriousness with which her little girl was accepting responsibility for her performance. And so the arrangements were made.

At three o'clock, her mother drove up in front of the school. Happy with the day's activities, Shelly came running to the car, her coat open and her long blonde curls blowing in the wind. In the car, a steady stream of chatter continued the full distance home as she reported all the excitement of the day, especially the detail about finishing her work on time. Into the house they went, and with music books in hand they were ready to leave when Shelly stopped. "Wait, Mom," and she led the way to her bedroom, where they knelt together by Shelly's bed. "Would you say it, Mom?" she asked.

Later that evening I called Shelly; knowing something of her concern for her lesson, I was anxious to hear her report. "Well, how did it go, Muffin?" I asked. With a happy, carefree voice she reported, "I did as well as I could for as much as I had practiced." This revealed immediately something of the wisdom in the prayer that her mother must have offered. It is love, tough love, that protects us against the ease that too frequently undermines our growth.

Love Makes the Difference

Women of varied ages from all parts of the nation were gathered together in one of the workshops of the general Primary conference held in Salt Lake City. I had accepted the invitation to conduct a workshop on positive classroom management—how to control children effectively while allowing them the necessary freedom to be responsible for themselves. Reviewing the writings of the experts yielded several outlines. There seemed to be ample information on the subject; however, if this workshop were to be effective and make a difference, I knew I must do more than just dispense information.

I had determined that everyone should be involved, allowing the wealth of experience from the many to become a resource for all. According to the plan, there had been good participation. With only twenty minutes remaining of the crowded two-hour session, the participants had now been divided into small groups of five to six each, where they were to glean from each other their best ideas. At the conclusion, each small group would select a few of the ideas to be shared with all the workshop participants.

I had responded to several hands that had been raised, joining each group just long enough to further clarify the assignment, which was, to exchange ideas on what it is that really makes the difference in a student-teacher relationship. Now while further ideas were being shared and friendships established, I moved toward the back of the room and observed. As I watched, a young woman about thirty years of age left her group and came over to where I was standing. She appeared to be rather shy and hesitant, and apologized as she asked if she might be the first one to respond to the entire group after the small discussions were completed. I was somewhat surprised at her request, because of her timid approach. Without waiting for my response, she began explaining: "When I was just a little girl, I used to walk to Primary directly from school along with all the other children. My mother and stepfather were not active in the Church and didn't seem to care a lot about me or what I did, so on Tuesdays, I would go to Primary." And then, as if to summarize the whole story, leaving out the many details she had obviously just relived after these many years, she said almost in a tone of reverence, "It was my teacher. She was the one who made all the difference."

I felt the intensity with which she spoke and waited to hear more. She continued, this time turning to draw my attention to the group of sisters in the far corner by the door. "See that elderly lady over there," she said, giving direction with her eyes and a nod of her head to avoid pointing, "the one with the glasses and the small hat?" I nodded. I had noticed her when she first came in. She was bent somewhat by her age, and I had marveled at her continued service. The young woman stood for a moment, her eyes filling with tears, as she swallowed hard and continued. "She was my Primary teacher. I haven't seen her since I was just a little girl. We moved away when I was quite young. I'm sure she wouldn't recognize me now." She hesitated a moment, and then said, "She's the one who made all the difference. I've thought of her so often over the past years as I've tried to guide my own children, especially since my call as Primary president."

As I watched the countenance of this young woman and listened to her story, I realized that this was the teaching moment that by comparison could pale all else that might have been said during the entire workshop.

At the end of the discussion time, as people began rearranging their chairs to participate again as a whole group, I made my way to the front of the crowded room with the young woman. She stood nervously at my side. I put my arm around her waist, hoping to assure her that she had done the right thing in asking to express her feelings to the entire group. After introducing her by name and explaining that she was married, had five children, and was the Primary president in a small town in Nevada, I stepped aside.

"I want to tell you about my Primary teacher," she began. All eyes were on her. I watched the reactions of the elderly lady in the corner, the one with the glasses and the hat. She looked, looked again, then leaned forward, squinting her eyes and adjusting her wire-rimmed glasses to allow her to peer over the top. I glanced back again at the young woman. Their eyes met for just a moment, and the elderly woman whispered aloud, "It is _____. It is," as she began getting up from her chair. It had seemed as though a great magnet was drawing these two souls toward each other. The space between them was quickly reduced, until they stood in the center of the room, embraced each other unashamedly, and wept. Everyone watched this human drama, waiting and wondering without understanding the power that had drawn them together.

The young woman turned to those seated in the classroom and simply said, "She was my Primary teacher." Then, looking again into the radiant, sparkling eyes of the wrinkled face, she said to her teacher as if in private, "I can't actually remember a thing you said, but I always knew you loved me, and it was knowing that that kept me going when I might otherwise have lost my way." Silence prevailed in the room, giving reverence to this sacred moment. With a returning awareness of the group, the young woman turned toward the audience, her arm still around the shoulders of the elderly woman, who was now wiping the tears from her happy face. As if by way of testimony, she repeated again, "I always knew she loved me."

The lesson had been taught; the time was well spent. Many wept silently as a final benediction was given on this great teaching moment.

The Frame and the Yarn

The scent of bayberry candles and burning pine boughs filled the air as we listened to the traditional strains of "Silent night, holy night, All is calm, all is bright." The firelight reflected in the faces of our immediate family. It was Christmas Eve and, according to our family tradition, each person could open one gift of his choice before going to bed. This year it would be especially difficult to choose since there had been so many secrets among the family, so much whispering, and so many closed doors, along with occasional shouts of "Don't come in!" It seemed that everyone knew something exciting that someone else wanted to know but must not find out before Christmas.

With the spirit of the season in such abundance, each one was suggesting that someone else be the first to open his gift that night. Little Shelly, who had made several trips over to the tree and back again, always looking in the same area, was now jumping up and down with excitement in her long, pink flannel nightgown. Grandma, sharing her anticipation, took things in hand by explaining to everyone that since Shelly was the youngest, it would seem only right that she should open her Christmas Eve gift first.

It was Shelly's seventh Christmas, and with eyes dancing, and in almost uncontrollable excitement, she pleaded,"Oh no, Grandma, please not me first. Let me say who's first."

Surprised by her obvious lack of concern for the many gifts addressed to her, everyone quickly agreed to do it Shelly's way and was curious to discover whom she would choose to be first. Without any hesitation, she stretched her arm full length, pointed to me, and said, "You be first." Not yet understanding her intent or why I should be chosen first, I moved on my hands and knees over closer to the tree, where I could better examine the gifts that I might choose from. Shelly was on her hands and knees at my side as I began the ritual of deciding which gift to open. No longer able to contain the risk of my making the wrong selection, Shelly jumped in front of me, reaching over all the gifts to a little package that had been carefully placed, half hidden by tinsel and a homemade ornament, between the boughs of the tree. To avoid even a moment's delay, she picked up the little package, which was wrapped in soft, white tissue paper somewhat wrinkled by what might have been frequent wrappings and unwrappings, as evidenced by the yarn that fit very loosely around the treasure. As if carrying out a well-rehearsed plan, Shelly, using both hands with great dignity, laid the gift on my lap. I reached out to hug the little gift-bearer, but she jumped back to escape any further delay.

"Open it, open it!" she cried. As the yarn fell free from the package, a squeal escaped Shelly's lips, and she covered her mouth by clasping one hand over the other.

Surely it is in giving that we find the true spirit of Christmas, I thought, as Shelly knelt again at my side. While my intent was to carefully open the precious gift by giving proper respect to even the wrapping, the excited little donor could not endure the waiting. Jumping forth and using both hands, she tore away the paper that had kept her secret too long. Holding the prize so close to my face, I was unable to distinguish it. I leaned back to better discern the gift before my eyes.

"I made it for you," she explained. "I made it all myself." Then, letting go of all that she had kept private for what must have seemed forever, she continued to expound on what had been her secret. "I got this frame with these nails around the edge, and then I got this yarn, and I wrapped it a special way," and finally, like a little eruption, she announced, "and it matches! It matches your kitchen!"

With Shelly still holding the precious hot pad, I wrapped her in my arms and wondered what else of any significance could possibly be under the tree—that is, except for one particular gift. It seemed as if it was taking Shelly's mother forever to unwrap the present she had chosen. She loosened the ribbon, then stopped, laying both hands across the large package on her lap while she joined in conversation that seemed to be causing unnecessary delay. I could feel my racing heartbeat, and with one arm around Shelly, I realized I was now experiencing the excitement of my secret that had been a long time in the planning.

It began with an old family heirloom, an oval picture frame that we all wanted but that was given to me. This old frame with its glass curved outward would be just the thing to safeguard some precious treasures, I thought. With careful restoration, it took on an elegance and charm made possible only by age and the family sentiment attached to it. Carefully I cut a piece of canvas the full size of the frame and, using light blue yarn, covered the entire surface with needlepoint. Near the top of the oval the letters L-O-V-E were stitched in a darker blue. In the center I had appliqued a small portrait of Shelly and her mother in their dark blue nightgowns, sitting together reading bedtime stories. A little pink ballet slipper, with the toe worn completely through by the spirited dancing of a three-year-old, also became a part of the collection, more treasured now than when it was new. A piece of her light blue Alice-in-Wonderland costume made originally for Halloween, then used as her official dancing gown, and now worn and torn, had been rescued along with a bit of tattered eyelet and placed among the treasures. Conspicuously near the center was a shiny blonde curl, tied with a bit of light blue yarn, from Shelly's first haircut.

The minute detail of this gift was vividly in my mind although the wrapping had not yet disclosed my prize. Uncontrollably, I reached out with one hand to assist Shelly's mom, exposing my reason for excitement. As she saw the gift and considered the full meaning of my offering, I began explaining. "I made it for you," I said. "You see, I took this frame, and then I got some yarn, and . . . "

Something about the sound of the words "the frame and the yarn" kindled a recall that echoed like a rehearsal from Shelly's performance. Through my own replay of this little experience came new insight, increased awareness, and a sensitivity to a teaching moment that had been staged by Shelly.

Oblivious for a few moments to the events around me, I pondered the meaning of this incident. Who was the teacher? Was she also the student? Was there only one who learned, or did each contribute to the teaching? Was anyone left out of the learning? Is not a teaching moment meant for all?

". . . neither was the teacher any better than the learner; and thus they were all equal, and they did all labor, every man according to his strength." (Alma 1:26.)

Make It Real

"Are you really planning to take the whole class on a plane trip over the valley?" asked the anxious mother as I picked up the telephone in my home one early evening. Before I could respond she expressed further concern. "It doesn't seem reasonable, and I'm concerned for their safety. Patty came home so very excited and she rehearsed all the details of your plan. It does sound exciting, but I must admit, her father and I are very apprehensive."

In an attempt to respond appropriately to a worried mother, I found myself struggling to keep the sound of laughter from my voice. "Mrs. Hansen," I began, "I can appreciate your concern, but—"

Her anxiety spilled over again as she interrupted, "Mind you, we are grateful for all you do for the children, but it's just the safety factor."

Once again I attempted an explanation, this time more directly: "We're not actually going on a plane ride, Mrs. Hansen."

There was a moment of silence and she responded in a less worried but more questioning tone. "But Patty said she had a ticket and was going to meet the plane and—"

"Mrs. Hansen," I interrupted, "let me explain. You see, children in the fourth grade, I find, are quite disenchanted with geography. It makes so little sense to them. They see no relevance, no meaning, and they really can't understand what difference the information makes to them. I thought that if there were some way for them to see the land formations from the air so that they could experience the lesson, it could make a great difference."

Again Mrs. Hansen's voice evidenced some concern as I heard a questioning "Yes?"

I continued, "We've been planning for this experience for some time. During the past few weeks, the children have made large maps of the major land formations in Utah. We have assigned reports to students who will serve as the guides and become experts on various areas. They will accompany us during the flight."

I heard still another "Yes?" ending in the same questioning tone.

"We have representatives from our class who have studied topographical maps, elevations, and rainfall reports. Others have become experts on industry, including Hill Air Force Base and tourism. Some hard-to-motivate boys have researched the fishing, hiking, and boating opportunities and will tell all about those during the flight. We'll have a slide show of the actual areas that we're supposed to be seeing as the plane takes off from the Great Basin area with the densely populated Wasatch Front below, climbs high above the Wasatch mountains, which form the backbone of Utah, and then flies east to the Uinta mountains, running east and west, and then on to the Canyonlands."

With that much explained, I waited for Mrs. Hansen's response. There was a long pause, indicating the possibility that she might have already been enjoying our flight. Finally she said, "I understand it now. It's just an imaginary trip, right?"

"Right!" I said.

"But wait a minute," she went on. "Patty said something about airsick pills, seat belts, stewardesses, and even lunch."

I smiled as I realized the effect of Patty's vivid report. "Mrs. Hansen, our room has been arranged as much as possible to look like the inside of an airplane. Our desks are in rows. We do have seat belts, mints for air sickness, even brown paper bags in case the mints don't work, and we have a movie aboard. Since we plan to be gone all day, the stewardesses appointed from our class made arrangements with the cooks in the kitchen, and school lunch will be served in flight."

"I guess Patty was right after all," her mother said. "You really are going to take a plane trip."

By now I began to feel the anticipation as I shared Patty's enthusiasm and gave further details: "We've recorded the sounds of a plane taking off and then in flight, all with the help of a hand mixer running at various speeds to give the needed effect. We also recorded the captain's voice, after we made the tough decision of who would get to be captain."

Mrs. Hansen seemed satisfied. In fact, had there been available seating on our plane, I believe she might have been willing to join our flight. I didn't hear from her again, but the following day—watching Patty lean steadily to the right in her seat as the captain's voice explained over the increased volume of the engines that we were climbing over the high Wasatch mountains, and if we looked to the right, we could see the heavily populated area below—I wondered if Mrs. Hansen might still question the reality of our flight when Patty reported her day's experience with the study of geography.

It was another day during the beginning of my first year of teaching. The subject of Utah history seemed too much to impose on those youthful minds so lacking in comprehension of time that they would sometimes ask me, "Were you with the pioneers when they crossed the plains?" The relationship of time and events has little meaning to children unless somehow it can be experienced, and so it was decided that within our class, we would have our own mountainmen—Jim Bridger, Jedediah Smith, Etienne Provost, and others. We would also have the various Indian tribes represented, and traders from St. Louis. There had been considerable research and reports and an effort made to locate buckskin jackets, traps, and beaver hats in preparation for experiencing a rendezvous—a big event when the traders from the East came with commodities to barter with the mountainmen in Utah for beaver pelts and other furs. The Indians were also a colorful part of the rendezvous, and this gathering, along with the trading, included many social activities. According to record, the mountainmen and Indians especially enjoyed wrestling while everyone watched the competition.

Each student prepared enthusiastically. Kevin Jensen became such an expert in recounting the tall tales of Jim Bridger and how he sailed his bull boat from the Bear Lake to the Great Salt Lake that when he gave his report it was as though he were reading it from his own personal journal.

The preparations for the rendezvous were complete, that is, as much as they could be with a class of twenty-eight students varying in degree of dependability, and the appointed day to experience the rendezvous had arrived. It was to be the last ninety minutes of the school day. During the last recess, the students had cleared the center of the room by pushing all the desks to the outer edge around the walls, which were covered with various displays.

At two-thirty, the historic event began. Each personality introduced himself in costume and shared with the class the documented details of his experiences. Much trading took place, and now it was time for the social activities. Several of the mountainmen and Indians had determined just who would wrestle together, thus demonstrating the rugged, tough, physical strength so much a part of both. Lots had been cast, the crowd had been moved back, and the first wrestle was on. Buckskin and feathers, cheers and laughter were all mingled together. It appeared that those standing along the side, many in costume, as well as those in the ring, were enjoying in a very real way the actual experience of a rendezvous.

I stood at the back enjoying the enthusiasm of the audience as much as the actual activity of the wrestlers—that is, until I turned to see the door to our classroom open. There, framed in the doorway, stood the principal. Words of explanation came flooding to my mind as I left the group with the boys still wrestling on the floor and hurried to give an accounting. It was the first time the complete disarray of the room had registered with me. The students were totally unaware of our unexpected visitor, and the wrestling continued. Before I could explain the significance of this historic event, the principal said in an authoritative tone, "Mrs. Kapp, I'd like to talk with you after school." His business completed, he left the room. As I then stood where he had been standing and caught a glimpse of what he had seen, I appreciated his waiting until after school to deal with this seemingly irresponsible teacher. Sometimes there might be a risk involved in following one's convictions, but it seemed to me that if a child could in some way experience an event, the whole story would have more meaning.

Before the children left that day, the room was orderly—each desk in place, books neatly arranged, sink cleaned, and boards brushed. Just as I was about to leave for the office with my explanation well rehearsed, the principal came again, this time into a tidy, attractive room. He smiled and said, "The boys told me about the rendezvous." Then he continued, "I appreciate what you do to make learning enjoyable." I'm quite sure that was not the speech he had planned to give originally, but I was grateful for the explanation the boys must have given to sell him on the benefits of this kind of classroom experience.

From that time on I knew I had the support of the administration. I felt little concern for any misunderstanding; however, I did wonder what the principal might have thought about the lesson we had had a couple of weeks before, when the Spanish explorers invaded our room, along with Father Escalante and Father Dominguez. Father Escalante was portrayed with great conviction by one of the Catholic boys in our class. As he walked across the front of the room in his dark robe and met the Indians encamped by the window, he stood to his full height and with great dignity began his message on Christianity. Immediately I sensed in this valiant young padre the intensity of his attempt to inform the members of the class who did not share the same religious background. It was his chance to express his deep feelings, and while religious education was not an approved part of the public school curriculum, we all experienced the conviction of a young boy who had something to say and needed to be heard by his friends that day. When we had the examinations that always followed an experience such as that, the response from the class indicated that everyone remembered the message from Father Escalante.

I found that it is much easier for children to learn if they can relate their learning to a real life experience. Geography and history became favorite subjects to the students I taught, but math had its own particular challenge, especially with Jimmy.

I first met Jimmy during my student-teaching experience. As I was introduced to Mrs. Ray's class as a student teacher who would be working with the children for about six weeks, I quickly surveyed the group, hoping to get a reading on their acceptance of me. In anticipation of my coming, Mrs. Ray had assigned each child to have his or her name printed on a card for his desk, large enough to read from the front of the room. Glancing quickly around the room, I noticed a desk at the back, away from the others, and a young boy sitting by himself. On his card in very irregular letters I read his name: Jimmy. He didn't look up. All the other students seemed curious, interested, some even excited, but not Jimmy.

The following day Mrs. Ray explained that Jimmy would be my responsibility. She explained that with two teachers in the room, I could take the time to give Jimmy special attention. "You see," she said, "he doesn't have a father. His mother isn't able to take care of him, and he lives with an aged, widowed grandmother. He doesn't get along well with the other students and is quite disruptive."

I looked up from the desk where Mrs. Ray and I were sitting and saw again the subject of our discussion. There he sat, in an old army shirt too large for his young body, sleeves rolled up to expose his dirty hands. He held in his left hand a broken pencil chewed off around the top. He seemed to be intently working at something.

"He always wears that army shirt," explained Mrs. Ray, "and he is incessantly drawing army pictures on his art papers and everything else. He draws tanks, guns, parachutes, and planes. He draws hand grenades, bombs, soldiers, and jeeps. I can't get him to do anything else."

During the next few days I thought a lot about Jimmy and about the battles he must be fighting within, seemingly alone except perhaps for the help of his grandmother. It was during math when the other students were busy with their work that I pulled up a chair and sat down by Jimmy. On his desk were many sheets of paper covered with sketches of tanks, planes, guns, and jeeps. His math book lay open on his desk to the wrong page. Multiplication, division, subtraction, and addition were of little interest to him. It appeared to me that the teacher's anxiety for "what was best for him" would have little effect on this young lad. If he could not leave his world of fantasy to come to us, then the possibility of entering his world in an effort to reach him seemed like a worthy endeavor. Not knowing where to begin I just said, "Jimmy, I would like you to tell me about your pictures." His immediate response indicated a questioning of my sincerity.

After testing me for a few days the way young children often do, Jimmy gradually began to allow me into his world. We talked about fleets of jeeps and the names of the planes. One day he told me that his shirt was the one that had belonged to his dad. Then, pointing to three blue stripes in a V shape, sewn with uneven stitches on his left shoulder, he said proudly, "These belong to me." I noticed that he changed his shirt only occasionally, but he wore the stripes every day.

During math each day, we would visit together for a few minutes. We began talking about numbers of jeeps and how many tires were needed to supply a fleet of jeeps. We talked about gas mileage and costs. We talked about numbers of guns and soldiers and parachutes. We subtracted demolished planes, and divided supplies to give equal portions to soldiers. I would check the math book for the day's lesson and replace the examples with things of importance in Jimmy's world. Eventually, he began asking for more and more and harder and harder problems.

With two teachers in the room, I could spend time with Jimmy in his world. When we began to speak his language, it seemed we found the key that unlocked his inner self. He seemed now to respond to math assignments and even to be more cooperative in other subjects. His actions were becoming less and less disruptive. By the end of the month, Jimmy's desk was in the third row from the back near the side and he was beginning to fit in. Six weeks seemed to pass very quickly, but within that time, strong feelings of friendship had developed.

One day toward the end of the month, when Jimmy was working faithfully on his own, he motioned for me to come to his desk. I leaned down, anxious to give what assistance I could. "Yes?" I said in a low voice.

"Could you come to Scout meeting with me tonight? I'm getting a badge and I'm supposed to have a representative. Could you be my representative?"

At that moment I knew we had bridged the gap.

By walking carefully into his world, I had been tested and finally trusted, and he had come to me. It was not until the last day of my assignment in that school, however, that I realized just how far Jimmy had come.

The class had planned a little goodbye party for me, and the last hour of school we had enjoyed a little program and then some punch and cupcakes. Cynthia had given a brief speech of appreciation and then presented a small gift, nicely wrapped. The children all watched as I opened the package. Before getting it open, I heard the full explanation about how they each had brought a dime and Marcy and Susan had been appointed to buy the gift.

With the little silver candy dish unwrapped and my thanks expressed, we began the individual goodbyes. From the corner of my eye, I watched Jimmy, who seemed to be purposely delayed at the drinking fountain. Finally, after most of the children had gone, he rushed forward. With his head ducked to avoid the embarrassment of a soldier in battle shedding a tear, he reached for my hand. Holding it in his left hand, he emptied the contents of his right hand into mine. Without looking up, he half whispered, "Don't forget me." Then he turned quickly and walked away. Glancing at the contents in my hand, I recognized three blue stripes, in the shape of a V. My eyes filling with tears, I looked up to see Jimmy going out of the door. On the shoulder of his shirt I could see the loose stitches of the black thread where his stripes had been.

Our Reputation

The substitute teacher had agreed to take my class for the day, and having reviewed my plans with her, I made a further comment before leaving. "I'm sure you'll enjoy this class. They are very obedient and respectful." Her smile suggested that my opinion might be that of a proud parent speaking of her child. I found myself justifying this statement by explaining that in our class we had talked a lot about shared reputation, and how every student in the class contributed positively or negatively to the reputation of all of us in Room 16. We had discussed our reputation as observed in the lunchroom and in the hall, on the playground and in assembly. We had all worked to build a good reputation, and I was sure she would find this class supportive and cooperative. She just smiled but reserved her comments until the end of the day when I returned.

"Mrs. Kapp," she reported, "you do have an obedient class and it has been a delightful experience." I could tell by the twinkle in her eye that there was more to the report. "Cynthia," she began, and with the mention of that name, I was ready to hear an exception to my statement on obedience. "During the last hour I asked the students not to leave their desks," she continued. "There seemed to be a lot of unnecessary moving about. Every student returned to his desk and remained in his seat, including Cynthia."

"Well?"

"Well, Cynthia remained in her seat by putting both hands under her chair and while in a sitting position held the chair to her as she continued to go from place to place!" We both laughed and agreed that every class should have at least one Cynthia, but perhaps not more. Our reputation might have been strained on that occasion, but not spoiled.

A few days later the children were getting settled after recess. A couple of them still lingered at the water fountain and the chatter from others gradually diminished as I stood near the door waiting for the last stragglers to come bounding in. They always had a very reasonable excuse—reasonable to anyone who understands that the ringing of a bell can't stop a runner on first base, or a turn half-played in tether-ball, or even an exciting story half-told by a ten-year-old. As I surveyed the class, only Bruce was missing.

Bruce had a brother who was just a year older. The brother's classroom was down the hall two doors to the right. These two boys, it seemed, were always looking out for each other, defending, pro-tecting, and sticking together. They had moved to the community just in time for the beginning of school, the last part of August, and already they had established a questionable reputation. According to the school records, Bruce's mother had passed away some years ago and his father was a traveling salesman. Bruce, along with his father and brother, had moved into an apartment complex in a location that hopefully might cut down on the travel time for his father, allowing him to be more available to the boys. In the absence of their mother, and most of the time their father also, the boys had developed an attitude of self-defense and a resistance toward authority.

I wondered what Bruce's excuse might be as I waited for him at the door. Just then two figures appeared, coming down the hall. The principal, exercising seemingly rightful concern, held Bruce captive by the collar of his worn jacket. Bruce was struggling to pull out of his coat in an attempt to get free from the authority that was in control.

"Does this young man belong in here?" the principal asked. At the beginning of the school year, I had asked him to inform me of any disciplinary measures to be meted out to any student for whom I had a responsibility. Mr. Carson had been faithful in honoring that request and was responding accordingly at this time.

I looked at Bruce with his young body straining to get away, his eyes looking a little frightened but more pathetic, an anxious expression that seemed to ask, *Would anybody claim me?*

"Yes," I told Mr. Carson, "he does belong in here."

"Then I'd like to know what you plan to do with him. His destructive conduct is quite unacceptable," he said. Giving a jerk on Bruce's collar, he continued to explain about the vandalism and the costly repairs caused by the boy's behavior.

The young victim quit his struggle as he risked interrupting the principal. "I can explain it, Mrs. Kapp, honest I can."

With this I realized that in his experience he seldom if ever had had an advocate, one who would listen and trust and allow him the chance to tell his story. "Mr. Carson," I said, "could I please assume responsibility for Bruce? He and I will talk it over and I'll report back to you."

The principal looked a little skeptical, but he finally let go of the boy's collar and commented as he turned to leave, "I'll expect to hear from you this afternoon on this matter." I agreed that he would.

Bruce and I stepped out into the hall together and I held his coat while he slipped out of it and then turned around to face me directly, not with his head dropped, awaiting the verdict, but with anxious and pleading eyes begging for a hearing. "Honest, Mrs. Kapp, I didn't do it," he said.

Bruce had been known in the past to misinterpret truth in his own attempt for protection, since he had no one else to speak in his defense. On several occasions his conduct had been questionable and frequently unacceptable. But without someone who cares, someone to teach and guide and love and discipline a child, who is really at fault? How does a child learn the boundaries without testing the edges and being secured by those who love him and establish restrictions?

"Bruce," I said, "you're in a difficult situation because of your reputation." With this accusation he dropped his head, feeling his appeal might be useless. "Can you see why Mr. Carson is so concerned?" He nodded his head as he looked at the floor. "Do you understand why he might think you were involved?" Again he nodded. He was not prepared for my next question, and he shrugged his shoulders hopelessly as I quietly invested some genuine concern: "What can I do to help, Bruce?"

I waited a minute, and we both leaned against the coatracks. The door to the classroom was closed, but we could hear Becky fulfilling her responsibilities as class president by giving instructions in the unexpected absence of the teacher.

"Bruce," I asked, "do you want to tell me about it?"

The chance that he might be understood seemed worthy of an attempt. Like a defendant on a witness stand, he began explaining in minute detail. "You see, I was standing close by."

"Did you see it happen?"

"Yes, I did," he said, looking directly at me. "But I wasn't even with those guys during recess. I was with Kevin." And with the discovery of the possible value of a witness, he said eagerly, "You can ask Kevin," and repeated again, "just ask Kevin if I did it."

"No, Bruce," I said, "I don't need to ask Kevin. I'm asking you."

"But he can tell you how it was," he said anxiously.

"Maybe he can, Bruce, but so can you."

With his story told, I asked one more question. "Bruce, why do you think Mr. Carson picked on you?"

"I know," he said, "it's my reputation." His voice made it sound like a dread disease, and I guess for him it had become that.

"Bruce, you can change your reputation if you want to, and I'll help you; but it will take a little time and you'll have to be patient and even understanding of people until they know you've changed." Again I waited and he waited.

The custodian walked by and smiled at me with a sort of "him again" look. I smiled back, knowing something that the janitor didn't know. A wounded spirit might at that very moment be in the process of healing. This possibility became evident when Bruce, with his eyes wide and hopeful, said in a very serious tone, "But what can I do, Mrs. Kapp?" I thought of the repeated offenses, although minor, of which this unguided boy had been a part. I realized some risk involved on my part, but thought of his future if he continued. "First, I believe, you must talk to the principal and explain." That appeared to be too much of a hurdle, and his expression immediately changed to one of doubt. I added, "I'll go with you, but you must do the talking."

"But what will I say?"

"Tell him what you have told me."

Then he responded in a pleading tone, "But Mrs. Kapp, he won't believe me."

"Why not?" I asked, hoping to make another teaching point.

"Because of my reputation."

"Bruce," I said, "maybe he won't, but if I defend you, I think he will believe me."

"Can we use your reputation?" he asked.

I smiled, thinking of the degree of learning that can take place at the right teaching moment. "Yes, Bruce, we can use my reputation, but if we do and then you fail to keep your promise, can you see what could happen?"

He was quick in his response. "Then I'd wreck your reputation, too."

"Yes," I said. "If that happens it could be that I wouldn't be trusted as a teacher, and if it got bad enough, I could even lose my job."

The risk must have seemed too great, and Bruce shrugged his shoulders again and looked at the floor. Putting my hand on his soiled and wrinkled shirt, I said, "I'm willing to take the risk for you, Bruce, if you are willing to accept the responsibility."

Together we walked to the principal's office. Just as we approached the door, Bruce looked at me for a little reassurance. I put my hand again on his shoulder.

Mr. Carson listened intently to the boy, glancing up at me occasionally with an expression of approval as I stood behind Bruce. With his case presented, the boy stood awaiting the verdict.

"Mrs. Kapp," the principal said, "are you willing to accept this report as the truth?"

Bruce turned for the first time and looked at me. I looked at him just a second before replying. Then in an unwavering response I said, "Yes," and

repeated again, "Yes, Mr. Carson, I am." The principal nodded in agreement.

Together we walked back down the hall to the
classroom. In an attempt to give a little reinforcement I said, "I was proud of you, Bruce. You did
very well. You told the truth and you were trusted."
With that he felt the need to reassure me. He
stopped to make his response: "I won't wreck your
reputation, honest."

As I looked at this young boy, seemingly so
alone in the world, I knew he wouldn't if he could
help it; but with so many challenges and so little
reinforcement and guidance, I felt concern, not so
much for my reputation, but for his. I guess he must
have known I'd be wondering, because on his own,
each day before leaving school, he would come and
make a report. Sometimes it was very brief. Other
times it included concern he felt for a group of boys
he found misbehaving, and he was anxious for me to
know exactly where he was and what he was doing
at that particular time. He would talk about his
reputation and mine, seemingly more concerned for
the latter. He always asked, "Am I doing okay?"
And I would shift the responsibility to him by asking, "Are you?" He would look me squarely in the
eyes and smile each time as he assured me that he
was.

The Witch Costume

A large package lay on the kitchen table, all wrapped, addressed, and ready for mailing. Before sending it off, however, Shelly's mother had decided she should check with her little girl. After all, it was Shelly's witch costume, and although she had always mailed her last year's costume to her younger cousins in Canada, it seemed only right to get her permission on this one also.

It was in the fall of the year, the time for cleaning cupboards and drawers and sorting out what to keep and what to discard. As Shelly's mother thought of the delight this fancy costume had brought her little girl last year, she wondered what the results of this year's costume might be. Having found a box just the right size, she had carefully lined it with white tissue paper, folded the lovely, long black cape with its high stiff collar, which had been made according to Shelly's specifications, and placed it in the bottom of the box. Next had come the full-length skirt, longer in the back so it would "trail behind like a real witch." The blouse, the cape, and the skirt, trimmed with just the right amount of silver glitter, had been added to the package, and then the tall black hat, with tassels streaming in sparkling splendor from the top, had been fitted carefully into the box. It was the long sash that bore the greatest remaining evidence of the dyed sheets that had been transformed into a "real witch's fancy costume." Now the box was wrapped and ready to be shared with other little girls whose eyes would dance as they opened the surprise package from Shelly.

Shelly arrived home in her usual happy mood, overflowing with her report of the happenings at school. At the appropriate time, her mother casually mentioned that the package on the table was to be mailed to her cousins and contained last year's Halloween costume. Shelly's response came as quite a surprise to her mother, since she had never hesitated about sending anything before—besides, she hadn't worn the costume for almost a year now.

"No, Mom, you can't send it," Shelly insisted, going straight to the box. "That's my fancy witch's costume."

With that, her mom attempted a selling job. "But Shelly, think about how happy it will make Becky and Jenny and Amy and Sarah, and you don't wear it anymore."

"But, Mom," Shelly explained, "I might," and then in an attempt to convince her mother, she quickly added, "and besides, maybe some of my friends will want to wear it for dress-up, and you wouldn't want my friends not to have anything to play in."

Shelly's mother realized that this was a matter that needed further discussion. Leaving her dinner preparation unfinished, she took her little girl by the hand and they sat together in the big chair. As her mother began, Shelly closed her eyes and with both hands over her ears, she said, "I don't want to talk about it." So they didn't. They talked about other things, until Shelly finally asked anxiously, "Mom, do I have to send my witch's costume?"

The response was reassuring to her. "No, my dear, you don't. I won't mail it if you don't want me to, but I'd like to talk with you about it. I'd like you to think about how you feel inside." With that, Shelly jumped off her mother's lap, stomped down the hall to her room, and closed the door.

In a little while her mother knocked gently on the bedroom door. "Who is it?" Shelly called, knowing she and her mother were the only ones at home.

"Your mother," came the answer. "I'd like to talk with you." She then waited to be admitted.

"Come in," came the voice from the other side of the door. The mother entered and sat on the floor beside her little girl.

"You really like that costume, don't you?" she began. Shelly, avoiding her mother's eyes, nodded. "Dear, I didn't realize that you liked it as much as you do, and I'm sorry if I made you feel bad." Again reassuring her, she repeated, "You don't have to give it away." Shelly felt relieved with this reassurance and the problem seemed to be settled, or so she thought.

Then, as if changing the subject, her mother began talking. "Shelly, you and I and Daddy are alike in a lot of ways." This seemed to attract her interest. Her mother continued, "We all have two spirits that try to influence what we do and how we feel inside." Shelly waited for more. "There is a spirit that wants us to be happy and feel good and to do the things that help others. When we think of others and share and help each other we feel happy. There is another spirit that wants us to be unhappy and selfish and miserable. Sometimes the decisions we make can make a difference in how we feel." She waited a moment, patiently, considering the possibility that some learning might be taking place. She then hugged her little girl, kissed her, and told her she loved her. She asked her what dessert she would like for dinner. Spudnuts were her favorite, and it was agreed that she should call her daddy at the office and ask him to pick some up on the way home.

A day went by and there was no further discussion about the costume. However, while vacuuming the floors the following day, her mother found the box under Shelly's bed, hidden by the dust ruffle that reached to the floor.

The following day when Shelly came from school, after her usual greeting and reporting, she left the kitchen quickly and closed the door, which was a bit unusual since the kitchen door was seldom closed. After about ten minutes, unable to control her curiosity any longer, Shelly's mom wiped her hands, left her baking, and went to the door. She opened it carefully. There on the floor in front of her was the big package. On the top was a note. The page was almost covered with a smiling face, and at the bottom was a note that read, "I love you, Mom."

Her mother, pleased because of the great message in that brief note, hurried to her little girl's bedroom. The door was wide open this time, and she was lying in the center of her bed with both feet in the air and a pillow covering her face. Her mother, hearing a giggle escape from under the pillow, grabbed the corner and quickly pulled it away to reveal a big smile and a happy and proud little face. After a big hug, her mother asked, "How do you feel inside, my dear?"

"Good," was Shelly's reply.

"How come?"

" 'Cause I did what I was supposed to do."

"You know, honey," her mother explained, "there was no way I could tell you before you made the decision just how you'd feel after."

Shelly hugged her mother tightly and then jumped off the bed. "What do you think they will say when they see it?"

Her mother replied, "I don't know what they'll say, but I think they will be happy."

About five days later in the early evening just after supper, the telephone rang. Shelly in her customary way picked up the phone and very properly announced "Larsens'," then waited a minute, looked confused, and handed the telephone to her mother. It was the operator. "Shelly Larsen, please. Long distance calling." It was only after Shelly had talked first to Becky, then Jennifer, Amy, and Sarah, and finally her aunt, that she realized the full impact of her decision. Aunt Shirley explained that one child was modeling the cape, another the hat, one the skirt and blouse, and little Amy, grandest of all, wore the long sash wrapped around and around her tiny waist. Finally, with the telephone replaced and Shelly no longer wondering "What will they say when they see it?" she threw her arms around her mother and rejoiced. "Thanks, that I could give my fancy witch's costume to my little cousins."

". . . for ye receive no witness until after the trial of your faith." (Ether 12:6.)

The Irrigation Ditch

The alfalfa patch was best of all, partly because it was located at the lower edge of our eighty acres by the grove of elm trees, and partly because of the irrigation ditch, its banks covered with yellow buffalo beans, which marked the boundary along the south side of our fields. But mostly, I think, it was best of all because of the smell. It is the recollection of that smell of alfalfa in the stillness of the early morning that brings every emotion of that occasion back over the years as clearly as though I were experiencing it for the first time. In the early morning, before breakfast, when one is fresh from sleep the smell is the very best.

Dad and I would often walk together through our fields. He would wear high rubber boots and carry a shovel over his shoulder, a long stem of wheat hanging from the corner of his mouth. I loved the way the heavy morning dew, still sparkling like crystals on the alfalfa leaves, would make our boots appear new and shiny with each step. As I would walk by his side, occasionally he would stop and pick up a handful of earth, almost reverently, then let it slip through his fingers as the breeze carried it gently to the ground. Looking upward into the cloudless blue sky, he'd say, "God's given us this good earth, but we must do our part," and then almost under his breath he would repeat, "We must do our part." It always seemed as if he were talking to someone but not to me, so I didn't feel the need to respond.

On this particular morning we walked together through the alfalfa until we stood side by side at the edge of the main irrigation ditch. We had not come this way before, and I didn't know the plan, but I had learned to watch and listen first and save questions for later.

Dad took the shovel from his shoulder and made his way down the bank of the ditch to the water's edge. Then he turned and, with one foot high on the bank, stretched his big hand toward me. Taking my hand in his, he steadied me until we stood together near the water.

I could often tell by the shape of his eyes and the angle of his chin the nature of the lesson he was about to teach, and I knew this was going to be "a good learning opportunity," as he always called it, quietly adding, "if your attitude is right."

"We're going to vault across the ditch," he explained. "I'll show you how."

I watched him as he reached with the shovel about to the middle of the ditch. He poked several times to avoid the rocks before he pushed the shovel deep into the bottom. Then, pulling the handle at an angle toward him, he took hold with both hands and swung forward, landing on the other side. "Like that," he said.

I watched carefully. I had one more chance to observe before it was my turn. He demonstrated again,
then returned to my side of the ditch.

Now was the time for the questions. "Dad, what
if I don't make it?" And he always saved his counsel
to use when it counted. "If you give it all you've got,
you'll make it." Then I noticed a slight smile as he
further counseled, "And if you don't, you'll land in
the middle and get soaked."

"And then what will I do?" was my next question.

"You'll still have to get to the other side."

With those options, it seemed important to try
hard to follow his first counsel. Dad didn't rush me.
It was as though he knew the crossing of the ditch
was maybe even more important than the water in
the ditch he came to use for irrigating.

I stood and watched. Suddenly there seemed to
be a vast audience encouraging me. The birds in the
elm trees nearby were chirping, almost as though
they were cheering. A big bumblebee that had been
weaving its way back and forth among the yellow
buffalo beans along the bank even joined in by buzz-
ing in a circle while casting a shadow on the water's
surface for water skeeters to dodge.

As I stood for some time watching those skeeters
skim the surface of the water, Dad offered his next
suggestion. "Honey, don't concentrate on the water.
You have to keep your eye on the bank on the other
side. It's keeping your eye on the target that makes
all the difference."

I guess he sensed my readiness and also the

proper timing as he slowly pulled the smooth handle of the shovel toward me and helped me get a firm hold with both hands. As if to say, "What do I do now?," I looked up and noticed Dad's straw hat hiding his wavy hair, his eyebrows forming a partial frame for the kind blue eyes that could look right through you. He smiled and said, "Give it all you've got."

With that, my hands tightened on the handle of the shovel. I paused a moment and then fixed my eyes on a particular clump of buffalo beans on the other side of the ditch that seemed to be standing at attention for this very moment. Taking a deep breath, I tightened my grip, glanced quickly at Dad, gave it all I had, and swung forward. I made it, landing right on top of the buffalo beans.

Quickly I turned to look back at Dad as he gave his usual sign for victory by clasping both hands together, raising them above his head, and shouting as though it were a glorious accomplishment. "I knew you could do it!" I watched then as he jumped the ditch with such ease that I wondered, "Why all the fuss just for me?"

It was a good morning, and by early afternoon we had cleared all the small ditches of any grass or weeds that might obstruct the free flow of the precious water. Dad paused now and pulled out his pocket watch, which was tied to his belt loop with an old shoelace. With a quick glance at his watch and then a look up at the sun, as if to check either his watch or the sun, I was never sure which, he announced, "Time for lunch."

We headed for the trees near the old granary. It was a familiar place. A narrow path had been worn through the grass leading toward the trees. In the middle of the trees, the tall grass lay flattened from many previous lunches. I sat down in a favorite spot as Dad separated the tall grass where our lunch pail had been placed to keep it cool. With the lunch pail opened, he removed his straw hat, the imprint of the inside band still on his forehead. He wiped his damp brow with one big sweeping motion of his arm. After a brief expression of thanks for the bounties of life, we were ready to eat.

It was the big water jug covered with wet burlap that I remember best. Something about the smell, that wet coarse texture so close to my nose, and tipping my head back waiting for the clear, cool water to touch my lips while Dad held the jug, made the whole event seem almost like a ritual. After I had my turn, Dad took his.

Following lunch, we'd stretch out on the soft, tall grass and look up through the trees. Sometimes I'd talk and Dad would listen, or Dad would talk and I would listen. As I recall it now, it seems as if Dad always listened as much as he talked, but this time it was my turn to listen.

"You know, Ardie," he said, "you learned an important lesson today."

I quickly agreed. "Yes, I learned to jump the ditch."

"Yes, you did," he said. Then he raised up on one elbow and asked, "Just how do you think you did that?"

That sounded like a strange question to me since he saw how I did it, but he seemed to want more, so I tried to explain. "Well, first I watched you, and then when it was my turn, I got a scary feeling inside."

That seemed to be the thing that he was after as he quickly inquired, "And then what?"

"Well, I just looked at the buffalo beans on the other side and tried real hard and jumped across."

As if to reinforce the lesson, he reviewed it again. "That's exactly right, Ardie. You had your eye on the other side and gave it all you had, and you made it."

Moving the support of his arm, he lay back on the grass and we watched in silence as the feathery clouds began to invade the blue sky. We could hear the birds in the trees, the distant moo of the cows, and the faint sound of the water falling over the drop in the ditch.

It seemed like quite a while until Dad spoke again, and then in a tone that remains with me yet. "Ardie, my dear," he said, "there are a lot of irrigation ditches to cross in life. Many of them you must cross alone." Then, as a final summary to his lesson, he repeated, "Keep your eye on the other side, give it all you've got, and you'll make it."